CW01467783

Everything Grows in the Valley

A Story of Redemption and Learning to Embrace Life's Adversities

Diana N Patterson M.Ed.

Copyright © 2017 by Diana N Patterson

All rights reserved. No portion of this book may be reproduced, scanned, or distributed in any printed, or electronic form without permission. Please do not participate or encourage piracy of copyrighted materials in violation of the author's rights. Purchase only authorized editions.

Editor: Terrie Scott

ISBN 978-1975657451
ISBN 1975657454

Printed in the United States of America

Dedication

This book is dedicated to every person who has suffered loss; who felt alone as they experienced the valley; who has struggled to find their way through the valley, and has yearned for or found redemption. Know that you are not alone love and there is beauty in the valley.

In memory of my beloved mother, Karrolyn Nita Edwards, who instilled strength and courage in me that allowed me to embrace the valley and travel into the light.

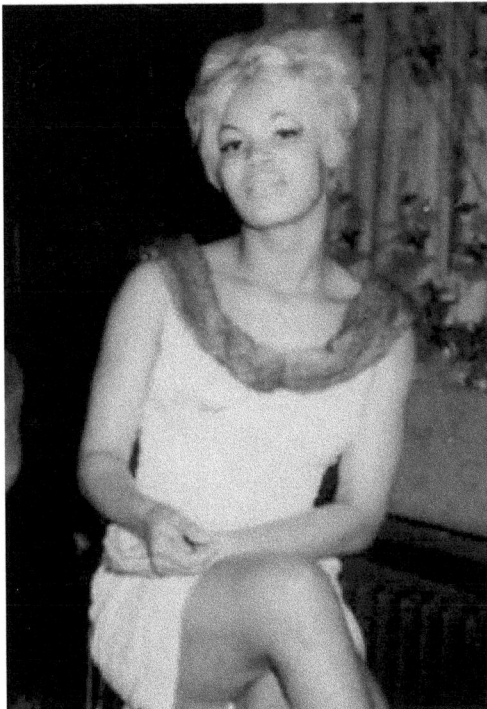

12/10/48 - 2/7/86

Acknowledgments

First and foremost, I want to give praise and honor to God for blessing me with the privilege and courage to share my story.

This book would not have been possible without the support and love of my four loving daughters, LaToya, LaTina, LaNisha, and LaShawna. You have been the wind beneath my wings, my guardian angels.

To my father, Joseph Horne Jr., you are my rock and my fortress. I would not be here without your constant encouragement, support, and love. Thank you for always seeing the best in me and believing in me.

To my brother, Pastor Joseph Horne-Edwards, who encouraged me and prayed me through the darkest times. Your spiritual guidance was God's expression of His love for me in action.

To my ex-husband Myron for giving me three of the most beautiful and loving daughters on the planet. In spite of our differences, you always believed in me and my capabilities, and you never allowed me to give up on my dreams.

To my aunts, uncles, other family members, and my godmother Melva who have always believed in me. Your love and support means everything to me.

To Michael, whose friendship, love, and support mean the world to me. Thank you for your constant encouragement and belief in me.

To my best friend, Laverne, who although she started her book years after I did, her courage to write her book and share her story gave me the courage to release my inhibitions and complete those last few chapters.

I want to extend a very special acknowledgement and thank you to my beautiful granddaughter Zariya for taking my vision for the cover of my book and creating such an incredible work of art. You are so amazing, my love.

Last but certainly not least, to my editor, Terrie Scott, your professionalism assisted in restoring something in me that I thought was lost forever. Your affirmation of my story...my truth....my pain... my everything, and the experience of being able to share it with someone who can connect on such a deep level has given me more joy than I could ever begin to properly express. I can't say it enough. Thank you so much for being a part of this journey with me. We are forever connected as sisters.

TABLE OF CONTENTS

Preface

Life, the word in and of itself, is subjective in context. How we live it, who we love, how we extend ourselves to others, what mattered to us, what is our purpose, and what will be our legacy? These are all questions that we examine to give our lives significance and purpose. As I was preparing to write this book, the question that consistently surfaced was what was my inspiration to the title of my book?

Back in 2009 I went on a cruise that ported in Victoria British Columbia in Canada, one of the most beautiful cities I ever bared witness to. The woman that shared my cabin with me was privy to the fact that I had never witnessed a mountain in person. I remember awakening to the sound of her voice screaming my name that morning as the ship made its way up the canal into Victoria. I ran to the balcony and was immediately overcome with emotion.

At forty-four years of age, for the first time, I was experiencing the majestic reverence of my first mountain. I stood there breathless, eyes filled with tears of joy, barely able to take in the awe and beauty that symbolized all of the majesty affiliated with a mountain. As I stood there gazing at this mountain, I can remember staring at the mountain's peak, thinking to myself why does the mountain top get all of the glory?

You see love, as I stood there and gazed upon the mountain top I did not feel the glory that so many esteemed as the mountain's greatest virtue. What I saw at the mountaintop was cold, barren, desolate, and lonely. Unlike so many others, the beauty that I saw was in the mountain's valley. When I looked at the base of that mountain, the valley, what I saw was life, birds flying, rivers steaming, and beautiful foliage. Everything that gave that mountain life flowed from its root and stood as the foundation of its greatness. Without the valley, the structure of that mountain could not exist.

I immediately paralleled the structure of that mountain with life's journey. During our valley experiences, we suffer tremendous adversity. We become so consumed with just trying to survive the experience that we don't take a moment to embrace the lessons and growth that comes with it.

In the same way, many of us focus far too much on achievements or goals, not the journey. Though there is greatness in achieving our aspirations, in the end the real significance, the aspect of the achievement that gives our lives the most meaning, is the journey that got us there. Too often we are in such a grind trying to reach the goal that we don't fully embrace the journey, the process.

Writing this book has been a five-year journey. There were times when I was writing feverishly with a natural flow that felt and appeared effortless and there were times when I would not write a word or even contemplate writing anything for months on end. For me, this was extremely uncharacteristic. Generally, when I aspire to do something I stop at nothing to complete the task. Ultimately, I realized there were psychological barriers that were obstructing my ability to finish this book.

From the inception of my journey to write this book I was immediately confronted with every fear, every critical comment, every judgement, every failure, and all of the self-doubt that made me feel unworthy and invalidated. I consistently asked myself, who am I to share my life with the world and why would anyone care? It was in those silent unspoken moments of every experience and every connection that I suddenly realized it was those very precious moments that were an affirmation to my existence. I am here, loving, living, and breathing each moment with every human being on this planet.

This is my truth and mine alone, one in which I am not ashamed nor for which I apologize. I came to realize this life was chosen for me and I for it and there is no shame in that. In fact, behind all of the hidden inadequacies, I found glory.

I contemplated for months and even into years as to whether or not to write an autobiography. The one point I was consistent about was that my book would be authentic and inspirational. The idea of writing an autobiography did not settle well in my spirit. I am not that transparent.

I remember reading Dr. Brene Brown's book, Daring Greatly (2012). Brene talked about how vulnerability requires boundaries and trust which allow us to share our feelings and experiences with people who have *earned* the right to hear them. Social media has taught me that the world can be very cruel and unforgiving.

Baring my soul and my life in a way that requires such a high level of vulnerability and transparency for me did not feel natural or safe. Ultimately what I decided was that it would be far safer for me to share a succession of my life's experiences in which *I* choose what I do and do not share and expose.

During my life's journey, I began to connect with some amazing people with whom I shared common experiences and what I began to realize is my story is not uncommon, that some of the greatest people I have met and some of the greatest people in the world all seem to share a common thread. That thread is redemption.

We have all survived experiences in which many of our counterparts would have collapsed and checked out on life given those same experiences. What makes us different? Is it merely our resilience or is it something innate within our DNA that allows us to survive in the face of some of life's greatest adversities and what did we learn along the way?

This book is my story, my life, my redemption.

Who Am I?

Define yourself as one radically designed by God. This is the true self. Every other identity is an illusion.

~Brennan Manning

Establishing our identity from birth is one of the most critical components to our existence and self-image. Without it we become vulnerable to others' opinions of who we are and lack a strong sense of our own self-worth. We allow ourselves to become victimized by a society that shames us into feeling unworthy, invalidated, and unlovable if we do not fit into the status quo. Starting our lives off with no distinction of who we are rocks the very foundation of our existence. We have no sense of meaning or worth in which to build ourselves on or to create a map in which to live our lives. It is as though we have been given a recipe with no ingredients.

My earliest memories were my life as a foster child. I was in foster care for a couple of years from the age of three to five years old, or at least that is the best I can make of what I have been told. My beloved mother Karrolyn Nita Edwards (12/10/48 – 2/7/86) had me when she was just fifteen years old, barely a child herself. During that time, I was not aware that I was a foster child. I just remember this amazingly beautiful woman that used to come and see me and bring me gifts and treats. I remember the excitement and joy I would feel when Louise, my foster mother, would tell me that my mother is coming to see me.

I don't think that I fully understood that the woman that came to visit me was my mother. I remember my mother's fragrance. She wore a perfume called Royal Secret and her scent would reverberate for hours after she left. I always felt this overwhelming sense of loss when she left as if I was missing a limb and would cry for hours sometimes.

My experience while in foster care was dark and cold. A child does not always remember a great deal about what people say to them or do for them. Through the lens of a child our memories are predicated upon what we felt in your presence and for me my memories of my foster home were dark and desolate.

As I was writing this book I struggled with exposing the molestation I endured from my foster brother Ricky. As I reflected on those dark memories I was overcome with shame. Tears began to stream down my face as I thought to myself, "Why do I feel ashamed?" I felt as though I had done something wrong. I was a four-year old child at the time who experienced atrocities that stripped me of my innocence.

At that moment, I realized how warped a society we live in that a child could be shamed to silence their precious little voices. Here it is almost fifty years later and I am paralyzed with fear at the thought of that level of transparency about my *victimization*, because that is indeed what I was, an innocent victim.

I remember one experience in particular when I was molested. My foster mother Louise often left me and my younger foster sister alone with my foster brother Ricky. Ricky was between twelve and fourteen years old at the time. I had become used to the routine and I knew what was going to happen when Louise left us alone. Ricky threatened to kill me if I told Louise what happened so I never exposed his indiscretions to her. I think Louise sensed that something was wrong with me that day. I became anxious and withdrawn as she prepared to leave.

I distinctly remember her asking me if everything was okay. I simply nodded my head as always. I ran to my bedroom and hid in the closet. I heard the door to the apartment close. The sound of Ricky's footsteps coming towards the bedroom mimicked my heart pounding as though it would burst through my chest. I knew what was coming so I hid my face in my hands praying that he would go away.

As Ricky's footsteps drew closer I trembled with fear and tried to hide behind some objects in the closet. Suddenly the door opened and Ricky was there towering over me like a lion preparing to attack his prey. I began to cry and scream begging Ricky to leave me alone. Initially he fooled me so that I would calm down, extending his hand towards me. Ricky gently took my hand and promised me he would not hurt me. His voice even felt reassuring. I took hold of his hand and walked out of the closet unaware that his only intent at that moment was to hush me up until he could get me out of the closet so that he could force me to do everything he commanded of me.

Ricky was extremely cruel that day and commanded that I do more than he generally demanded me to do. Instead of the normal fondling my vagina with his fingers and making me touch his penis he wanted more. Ricky grabbed me by my hair and pulled my face to his penis and commanded me to open my mouth. I started gaging and screaming but he just pulled my face closer to his penis and forced it in my mouth and thrust back and forth with force threatening to kill me if I moved.

I was overwhelmed with fear. It probably only went on a few minutes but it felt like an eternity. When Ricky was finished, he began to urinate in my mouth. I somehow managed to hit Ricky in the stomach and broke away from him. When it was over I curled up into a ball in the corner of my room crying until Louise came home.

As I was lying there crying, spirit broken, I just remember crying out for someone, anyone to help me. I remember thinking something was wrong with me and that I was a bad little girl. Living in fear of Ricky's indiscretions had become my normal. I don't know why I felt like it was my fault but I did. Ricky deprived me of my innocence and I was never the same after that.

Louise found me in the corner overcome with fear and despair at what I had experienced. She asked me what was wrong in a stern callous voice. Instead of consoling me she yelled at me and told me to go to bed until I stopped crying and told her what was wrong with me. I laid there in fear crying, thinking about the beautiful woman that would visit me, hoping she would come and rescue me from my foster home.

As with all fairytales, my wish came true and my mother came and took me away from my foster home in Milwaukee, Wisconsin when I was five years old and moved me to Madison, Wisconsin. When I arrived at my new home in Madison I was immediately greeted by my little brother Joseph who was the joy and love of my life throughout my childhood.

As much as my mother loved me I became confused about my identity. Who was this beautiful woman and how was I connected to her? Who was my foster mother and why did I call her Momma and where was she? My mom was married at the time to my (stepfather), my daddy. Who was this man and why did my brother call him Daddy? I felt comfortable and even happy with my new family. However, I felt a sense of disconnect and loss because of the new life I began and the old life I left behind. Although the old life bared nothing but pain, the unfortunate truth was it was my normal and within me lied a peculiar sense of loss.

The influence other's opinions have on a child's self-perception can be crippling in a child's ability to view themselves outside of their lens. When my mother and father needed a babysitter, they left my brother and I with one of my mother's best friend's children. They would babysit me and my little brother quite often. Some of the younger siblings in that home were very cruel to me and teased me repeatedly calling me cruel names. I remember one experience in particular when they were babysitting me and my brother. They were always mean to me, but even more than usual that day. They kept picking on me and taunting me, calling me cruel names like monster and telling me that Joseph was not my brother and my parents were not my parents, insisting that my parents did not love me. For a child, it was devastating.

My little brother, who was no more than two years old at the time and undeniably protective of me, yelled at all three of them crying and shouting, "Leave my sister alone!"

My brother and I were already close but in that moment a little bit of that disconnect that I was feeling when I first moved to Madison was instantly dissolved. I was redeemed and I felt like I belonged to something special. I had never felt as loved as I felt in that moment. My earliest experiences set the foundation for what would prove to be a journey in which I was always trying to embrace and figure out who I was and what I wanted in life.

Unlike so many, I did not have that spiritual foundation that so many have in which they can relate their identity to God. I was not raised as a Christian. My parents were wonderful human beings, but they were married young and did not go to church. What I do remember is that they were always helping people and extended kindness and love to anyone in need.

God has a way of letting us know his presence is amongst us, even when we have no clue who He is. Although I did not know God, I *knew* God and somehow, I knew that God knew me. I always felt as if I had a guardian angel watching over me, protecting me. As I reflect on those times, I recognize our innate need to understand our identity. Although, in my opinion our identity is our birthright, society constructs us to believe it is some external force that is awarded to us based on our socioeconomic status.

Our identity is the very essence of who we are. I believe the most important characteristic a parent can instill in their child is a strong sense of identity and the way we do it is through our actions. Unfortunately, when our children are born we do not get a parent guide or handbook on how to raise them. We are going to make mistakes, have faults, imperfections, and flaws in our character.

I would contend that our vulnerability and humanness is the component that will foster the type of relationship necessary to truly connect with our children. Our willingness to say, "You know what, I messed up, I am not perfect, and most importantly, I'm sorry," is all our children need to feel validated and loved without prejudice or judgement.

We teach our children how to love themselves by loving ourselves, flaws and all.

Who am I? I am Diana Nita Patterson daughter of Karrolyn Nita Edwards and Joseph Horne Jr. Although Joseph Horne is not my birth father, he *is* my father. I would be remised not to give mention to my birth father Walter Harrell and thank him for his contribution to my existence. I am a woman, mother, and grandmother who was created in God's image, a descendant of Abraham, molded and created by the hands of God, predestined for greatness.

Motherless Child

I wonder if my first breath was as soul-stirring to my mother as her last breath was to me.

~Lisa Goich

There is no greater suffering than to feel the agony of bereavement while your loved one is still alive. My beloved mother Karrolyn Nita Edwards died when I was only twenty-one years old, she was thirty-seven at the time, but our relationship as mother and daughter died years before she died. My brother Joseph was only seventeen when my mother died.

It's interesting, I see my life in two phases, my life before my mother died and my life after my mother died. The entire foundation of my identity, my existence was shattered after my mother's death. I was so young and still trying to figure out who I was and what I wanted in life and in an instant, she was gone.

My experience with my mother has caused me to become very sensitive about the bond between mother and daughter. The mother/daughter relationship entails very special dynamics. The relationship has the capacity to be very beautiful and close or stressed and distant. Complicated at times, this relationship requires consistent nurturing in the same way we grow a plant. If it is not consistently nurtured and pruned, it can collapse and wither with time.

There was an ocean of tears that came with this chapter. I struggled with how to present this chapter in a way that gives my mother the highest honor, one that she well deserves. My mother loved me with all of her heart and everything that is beautiful and amazing about me came from her, but unlike so many mother/daughter relationships my mother and I did not share that close bond.

In fact, there were times when I did not think my mother liked me at all. It was difficult to understand our relationship experiencing it as a child. What I know is I have these painful memories that are permanently inscribed in my soul that are as raw today as they were in those moments when I experienced them. They come with a sea of unresolved emotional trauma that long for my mother's touch, her voice, and her reassurance for healing and closure.

A mother's love is as infinite as time. It has the capacity to love us beyond our pain however, there are circumstances in which the fragility of a mother/child relationship can be rocked off the core of its foundation. I do not quite remember when I began to feel disconnected from my mother but there are a few memories in particular that are engraved in my memory like an old photograph.

As I reflect on my childhood, I do not have any memories of mother/daughter moments where it was just me and mother out doing things together, enjoying one another's company. I read something once that talked about how easy it is to remember the negative experiences we endure in life and how difficult it is to focus on all the good things.

I spent a great deal of time contemplating on whether my truth, my memories, are a distortion of reality. What I realized is most of my experiences with my mother were during my childhood so my perception of our relationship was through the lens of a child. In truth, I did not have the mental or emotional capacity to understand what my mother was experiencing as a woman and the impact that it had on our relationship.

I will be sharing a few moments from my childhood in which I have experienced brokenness, pain, and disconnect from my mother. These memories are as raw today as they were back then. Opening up about such personal moments involving my mother and I required a tremendous amount of courage. With all of the apprehension that I am feeling, I am convinced it is necessary for my healing. Unfortunately, my mother died before I had an opportunity to tell her I was hurting.

My first painful memory happened when I was about twelve years old. I was well developed for a twelve- year old. I was at that awkward age when I was starting to develop and my body was changing. I had beautiful caramel skin, no acne, a slim waist, my breast were kind of small but proportioned with my body, I was blessed with a large behind but not too large, just right in fact with hips to match. I had not quite figured out my hair yet but I often searched through beauty magazines searching for hairstyles that suited me. I was very intelligent and articulate. I was an excellent student. I would not say I was shy but I kept my social circles small and I was very particular about who I allowed to get close to me.

I had a very close friend who was in foster care at the time. She often ran away from home. She was a lot like me in many ways and she did not allow anyone to get close to her but me. I wanted her to come live with us but my parents had no interest in becoming foster parents at the time.

My mother was cognizant of the problems parents can have sharing a phone line with an adolescent child so they allowed me to have a private phone line in my bedroom. It came with some very stern rules, one being that I had to be off the phone by nine o'clock on school nights. I made sure I was respectful of my mother's curfew because I was fully aware of the consequences if I did not abide by my curfew.

One freezing wintery night my phone rang a few minutes before my curfew. I remember that day because it was freezing outside. My bedroom window was covered with ice from the blistering cold. Sub-zero temperatures were common in Wisconsin. I answered my phone and it was my best friend. She was crying frantically, so much so I could hardly understand what she was saying.

I could hear the brisk wind beating the phone and I could hear her voice trembling as though she was freezing in the bitter cold night air. I was concerned and remember feeling an overwhelming sense of wanting to help her. She did not know where she was but she told me something happened at her house and she got into an argument with her foster brother and her foster mother slapped her. She said her nose was bleeding and she was freezing and could not feel her hands.

My parents were not home so I was trying to find out where she was so that I could call the police and try to get her some help. She kept trying to describe her surroundings and any landmarks but the longer we talked the more upset she became. I remember her screaming and telling me her fingers felt like sharp knives where inside them.

At that point, we had been talking for well over twenty or thirty minutes. As I was on the phone with her I heard my bedroom door open and my mother burst in my room and snatched my phone away from me and asked me what the hell

I was doing on the phone after nine o'clock. I was trying to explain what was happening to my best friend. My mother was screaming at me so it was difficult trying to explain to her why I was on the phone after my curfew.

My mother snatched my phone out of the wall and stormed out of my bedroom. I walked out of my room behind her because I was still worried about my friend and I felt my parents would help her if they knew what was going on. I went into the living room to try to explain why I broke my phone curfew.

My mother was huge on respect and did not tolerate talking back to her at all. I was frustrated because my mother kept yelling at me and would not give me a chance to explain what happened. Before I knew it, my mother screamed "Shut the fuck up bitch!" and grabbed my only school picture, tore it up and threw it on the floor.

I still remember seeing the small fragments of my picture all over the living room floor. It was my seventh-grade school picture and the only picture my mother had of me at the time.

I was devastated and confused. My mother had never called me out of my name before. I ran to my room, cradled my pillow, and cried myself to sleep. I felt this ache in my soul, an emptiness like I was out in the wilderness alone, cold, and hungry.

Amidst all of my pain I remember still worrying about my best friend. Where was she? Was she okay? I woke up the next morning to get ready for school. My eyes were so puffy from crying all night that they were almost closed shut. I remember feeling like my mother hated me and thinking how I was just trying to help my friend.

That was the first time I felt so distant and disconnected from my mother. We never went back and talked about what happened so my emotional scars never had an opportunity to heal, they just sort of festered over like a bad sore. This was the beginning of the deterioration of me and my mother's relationship.

The next painful memory happened when I was pregnant with my oldest daughter LaToya. I was only fifteen years old at the time and her father and I had been dating for about a year. I can remember the disappointment on both my parents faces when I told them that I was pregnant. My oldest daughter's father was a teenager himself. He was verbally and physically abusive towards me and as expected my parents did not like him and did not want me to date him.

I will discuss my relationship with him in a subsequent chapter. A painful truth in my life is that my relationship with my oldest daughter's father contributed to the demise of my relationship with my mother. Both my mother and father knew my capabilities and my gifts. I was not living within my full potential, in my home that was an expectation.

My family was evicted from our apartment and we had to go live with one of my dad's best friends for a couple of days. I did not like my dad's friend because he beat his woman. I remember my dad and mom getting in the middle and protecting her many times. My dad's friend was an alcoholic and he was generally very nice to me so there was no way I could have seen what was coming.

One day my dad's friend was alone at his apartment with me and my little brother. My parents were both at work. My dad's friend had been drinking and he was harassing me. Initially it just started off with him asking me a bunch of annoying questions but at some point things shifted drastically and he started trying to grab me. I demanded that he keep his hands off of me, but he just grabbed me by the neck and tried to pull me close to him.

In that moment, I felt like the child that was molested by my foster brother and my instincts told me to get out of there as soon as possible. I kneed my dad's friend in his groin area and took off running as fast as I could. It happened in the dead of winter and as far as I can remember the temperature was freezing outside and the ground was covered in snow. I had on a short-sleeved maternity blouse and no coat but I was running so fast that I never once stopped to think about how cold it was outside that day, I just kept running as fast as I could trying to get to safety.

My oldest daughter's paternal grandmother, Bunchy, lived about three miles from my father's friend. I kept running trying to get to her house. I don't think it hit me how cold and afraid I was until I got inside of Bunchy's house. I was crying and frantic when I got inside her house. She just grabbed me and hugged me and asked me what was wrong. She could tell something horrible had happened to me.

I don't think I was in Bunchy's house over ten minutes before my mother knocked on her door looking for me. Bunchy let my mother in and she immediately started yelling at me and asking me what the hell I was doing there. My mother told me to stay away from Quintin, because she was concerned about Quintin hurting me and my unborn child. She assumed that I came to Bunchy's house to see him.

I began to explain what happened to my mother and she started screaming at me calling me a liar. Bunchy tried to intervene and tell my mother what happened to me and why I was there but my mother had it with my excuses about Quintin and before I knew it she slapped me in my face so hard I fell back and my nose started bleeding. Bunchy started crying and begged my mother to listen to me, but my mother wasn't trying to hear it and she just grabbed me and we left.

After my mother and I left she went off on me again and told me there would be more consequences if I continued to go around Quintin. I didn't try to explain anything else to my mother because I knew she wouldn't believe me. She was fed up with my lying and sneaking around to be with Quintin and had lost all trust in me.

The next incident happened about a year after my daughter was born. My family was evicted from our home. I remember my mother approaching me when I was at the park. She walked up to me emotionless and told me that we had to move and that I could not move with them.

I stood there in shock and disbelief. I had a daughter and nowhere to go. I just stood there for what felt like an eternity. At the time, I felt like my mother did not want me or love me anymore but in hindsight I came to realize it was time for me to grow up and this was something my mother prepared me for. I was going to be eighteen soon and I had a child. I would soon become an adult and I needed to create a life plan so that I could be the mother that my precious daughter deserved.

After the shock settled in, I began a relentless search to find a new home for me and my daughter. I moved in with very dear friends of our family that were more like family, in fact I called them Uncle Joe and Aunt Cindy. They took both my daughter and I into their home. I matured a great deal through that experience, I had to.

During the time that I lived with Uncle Joe and Aunt Cindy, my mother stopped speaking to me. Tears are flowing down my face as I am writing this. It is strange, I felt like I experienced my mother's death before she died. I do not remember why my mother stopped speaking to me nor do I remember doing anything that should have warranted her not speaking to me. I remember many nights waking up in the middle of the night with a pain that I felt in the very core of my soul. I longed for my mother's voice, her beautiful smile, her strength, her fragrance.

I would curl up in a fetal position in my bed and hold my daughter as though it was the last time I was ever going to hold her. With tears streaming down my face I would stare at her for hours. She was so innocent and beautiful. I never wanted her to experience the pain I felt in that moment. I wanted to give her the best of me and raise her in a way that shielded her from all the pain she would endure in her lifetime.

One afternoon my mother came by the house where I was living because Uncle Joe was working on her car. I was downstairs when I heard the doorbell ring. I ran upstairs and answered the door. I was surprised to see my mother at the door. At that point, it had been several months since I had seen my mother. It is difficult to comprehend how you can live so close to someone you cherish and love and feel as though you are continents away from them.

I was overcome with joy as I opened the door and saw my mother standing there. I recall the excitement and joy I felt in that moment. I looked at my mother and extended my arms out to hug her and said, "Hi momma!"

My mother just brushed past me as if I was invisible and asked me where my Uncle Joe was. She did not even look me in my face. Perhaps it was my pride or perhaps fear of further rejection, but I did not want my mother to see me fall apart so I waited until she left and went to my room and cried for hours.

I was overwhelmed at the level of rejection that consumed me in that moment. I had never felt as alone as I felt that night. All I remember is that I felt as though I was afraid of the dark and someone tossed me into a black hole and left me there to die.

I fell into a deep depression after that. This was my first *valley* experience. It was in those moments when I felt abandoned, alone, unloved, and unworthy of any amount of joy that life had to offer me that excavated me to a higher level of self-consciousness. I reached deep within myself to find my worth, my purpose in life.

Every time I gazed into my daughter's beautiful hazel eyes I felt an overwhelming sense of purpose and meaning. *I had to survive* for her. I was not going to allow this experience to consume me with darkness. I reached deep within myself and realized I had a choice to either allow this experience to extinguish my light or allow my light to consume the darkness. It was so much deeper than an aspiration to succeed, I *needed* to survive for my daughter.

My relationship with Quintin put a tremendous strain on my relationship with my mother during my adolescent years and I know it disappointed her tremendously for her to treat me the way she did, but there were things that happened between me and my mother before I ever got involved with Quintin that hurt me, and I did not understand.

In truth, to this day I wish I could ask my mother what happened. Why was she so angry with me? What I know is that experience motivated me to aspire for something greater. So often this is the point where we choose to give up, we stop climbing the mountain.

We are overwhelmed with the journey to make it to the top. We stop believing in ourselves because we allow one moment to dictate a lifetime when in reality regardless of the pain, it is indeed a moment, a moment that shall pass.

I felt this sense of urgency to put the fragmented pieces of my life back together. I had to make it for my daughter, she depended on me. I made the decision to go to college. I knew it was the key to my success and building a strong foundation to raise my daughter. My Aunt Cindy was instrumental in my decision to go to college. She spent her days helping me make the decision on which college to attend and helped me fill out applications. I decided to attend the University of Wisconsin-Milwaukee which was about seventy-two miles from Madison.

I knew my success in college would be a lot more difficult with a child. My daughter LaToya was three years old at the time. Although my mother and I had not really been speaking, I went to her after I received my letter of acceptance to UWM. That was the first time in as far back as I can remember that I could tell my mother was proud of me. All she ever wanted for me was to be successful in life.

My mother and I decided that it would be best that I leave LaToya in Madison for at least my first semester. My mother and my daughter's paternal grandmother agreed to help me with LaToya. I appreciated my mother and Bunchy so much for allowing me to leave so that I could build a better life for me and my daughter.

Things went well for a while and then I received a phone call from my mother one day. I'll never forget the tone in her voice. She said, "Diana, come and get your daughter."

I can't explain it but I could tell by my mother's tone that I should just do what she said with no questions and I came and got my daughter that weekend. My mother was concerned that my daughter's paternal grandmother was going to try to take custody of my daughter. I wasn't sure how LaToya and I were going to make it but somehow, I knew we would be alright.

It was the spring of 1985. My oldest daughter and I were still living in Milwaukee. I received a phone call from my mother that would change my life forever. They say there are moments that happen in our lives that remain engraved in our memory like a well-crafted sketch, for me that was the day.

I answered the phone and my mother said, "Diana I have something to tell you." I remember this chill going up my back and traveling to the nape of my neck. Before she ever said anything, I began to tear up because I could hear in her voice that something was wrong.

My mother said, "Diana, I have cancer." In that moment, it felt like the world stopped and there was nothing but silence everywhere. My heart felt as though it was going to drop to my feet. I stood there stunned and shaking. I asked my mother if it was serious. My mother being the protective woman that she was tried to reassure me that it was not serious and that she was going to be fine but something in my spirit told me different.

My love for my mother grew through that experience and our bond as mother and daughter grew closer. We had lots of good talks during my mother's illness but somehow, I could never bring myself to tell my mother about the painful memories that I had. I guess in many ways I was protecting her in the same manner she protected me when she told me she was not going to die.

In that moment, the only thing that felt right was being present and honoring the time I had left with my beautiful mother. She was so strong and courageous and she fought to the finish.

It was February 7th, 1986 when I stood over my mother, eight months pregnant with my second daughter LaTina at St. Mary's hospital in Madison, Wisconsin and watched my mother take her last breath. My mother was surrounded by me, my brother, my father, and her sisters and brothers when she departed this life.

That was the worst day of my life. The pain I felt in that moment felt like it could have literally taken me out of here. Living without my mother felt impossible and I remembered feeling angry because we were finally close and then she died.

The painful truth is when my mother died that little girl inside of me ceased growing. It's as though I was frozen in time and that little girl who needs her mother is still inside of me screaming and longing for my mother's love.

All I know is I needed her then and I still need her now. Nothing, and I do mean nothing, can prepare anyone for the loss of their mother. Sometimes when I think about it, it appears to parallel the experience an infant endures during childbirth when they are extracted from their mother's womb.

That time between when they are born and held in their mother's arms for the first time must be an extremely traumatic experience for the infant.

In many ways, it seems Christ felt that same disconnect on the cross when he felt God had forsaken him. The trauma affiliated with that level of separation can damage an individual beyond repair if they are not properly nurtured through it.

As I previously mentioned, writing about my experiences with my mother was a very difficult decision for me. I do not want anyone to judge my mother, the experiences we had were not who she was, they were what we went through. I never talked to anyone about my experiences, not even my family until recently mainly because of my concern about people's perception of my mother.

My mother was an extremely beautiful, strong, and wonderful human being and all of my friends adored her. My parents also became foster parents when I was young and made a difference in the lives of every child that was brought into our home. I have no doubt in my mind that if my mother were still alive today we would have a beautiful relationship, but I owe it to myself to live my truth and express my experience through *my* lens and what the experience felt like for *me*.

I often felt like my mother did not like me and even hated me at times. Because we never discussed it, I was left with broken fragments of my life that had no answers.

A residual of my experiences with my mother has caused me to become very sensitive and protective about mother/daughter relationships. There are many women that still have their mothers or their daughters and they don't even speak. My purpose for this chapter is to strengthen the mother/daughter relationships of my readers, those of you that still have one another.

For the mother's, it is imperative that you listen to your daughter's and open up to them in a way that they are not shamed into silencing their voice from being able to openly express any pain or wounds they have regarding their relationship with you. When you listen to them, listen with your heart and understand that their perception of the events that took place happened through an entirely different lens than yours.

For the daughter's, please know that in *most* instances our mother's genuinely love us. We do not have the capacity to see inside our mother's hearts and feel what they are going through and what events in their lives impact how they raise and deal with us as their daughter's. While you are still here and able to openly express your pain, talk to your mother's and give them an opportunity to give you the answers you need to heal and move on.

Because of my experience with my mother, last year I gave my daughter's an opportunity to sit down with me and express any unresolved pain with me. During some of my recent conversations with my daughters as painful as it was to hear, I discovered that my daughters were dealing with some unresolved hurt and pain in their relationships with me.

I used that as an opportunity to heal my babies' wounds. I sat down with all four of them, paper and pen in hand and Kleenex nearby and listened with my heart. It was terribly difficult hearing some of the things I did and some of the decisions I made over the years that hurt them and affected them, nevertheless I respected their views and we talked about it.

I begged my daughters not to allow me to leave here without helping them to heal and told them how important it was that I was a part of that process. It was difficult but beautiful and our bond as mother and daughters are stronger now than it has ever been. Hearing their perspective was eye opening and such a contrast from mine. As much as it hurt to hear some of it, it helped me to understand some things about me and my mother's relationship, something that I needed.

It appears that we have an innate tendency to allow what happens to us to become who we are instead of what we experienced when in fact it is an experience that happens, a moment in our life, a moment that evolves into the next moment. We must learn to embrace the idea that each new moment in our life is a new beginning and each moment that passes should be left exactly where it is, in the past.

We have the capacity to propel ourselves to a life of fulfillment if we will just allow ourselves to understand that the challenge we face in the valley is continuing to move forward while embracing all of the beauty that surrounds us as we walk through it.

Bruised Innocence

Enjoy the peace and freedom that comes from leaving.
~Domestic Violence Survivor

I can't say he was my first love, but he was my first boyfriend. At the tender age of fourteen I had no clue what love was. I was a good student and worked as a peer counselor for the community center near my school. I had beautiful smooth caramel skin, a pretty face, shoulder-length hair, and an hour glass figure. I was confident, intelligent, and articulate. At the time, I was more focused on school and the community than boys. His name was Quintin and he was pretty much everything I wasn't. He was not a good student and he hustled on the side to make money and I would later find out he smoked marijuana as well.

When I met Quintin, I did not know anything about him except that he was a pest and would be waiting for me on his ten speed bike when I got off the bus from school or work quite often. I was extremely annoyed with him in the beginning. Quintin was kind of cute. He had slanted Chinese eyes, plump lips, sandy brown hair, and he was pretty muscular. Quintin kept himself up and he always dressed nice.

Generally, when I would step off the city bus he would follow me to my apartment building on his ten speed. He would strike up friendly conversation as he was trying to implement his plan of action as to how he was going to get me to agree to go out with him. Quintin had this hustler demeanor that turned me off, but underneath it he was actually really nice. Sometimes he would have flowers, candy, or stuffed animals for me when I got off the bus. Over time I opened up to him more and more.

A few months later, Quintin invited me to his uncle's house to meet him. I was a little nervous about going but I agreed to walk to his uncle's house with him. My knees were shaking all the way over there for fear Quintin was going to try to make a move on me. When we got there I met Quintin's uncle, his uncle's girlfriend, and a couple of his cousins. They were very nice to me. Much to my surprise Quintin was very sweet and respectful during my entire visit.

On the way home Quintin held my hand and I let him. When we got to my apartment he said, "So how would you feel about being my girlfriend? I think you are so beautiful."

I stood there stunned. I mean I liked him and he was really nice, but I did not want a boyfriend. I told Quintin I would have to think about it. He just kept asking me every day for a few more weeks until eventually I just said yes so he would leave me alone, but he didn't.

Things were pretty good in the beginning. Quintin was always buying me nice things and he was very attentive towards me. My parents were strict, so we did not have the opportunity to spend much time together alone. My parents did not seem too impressed when they met Quintin.

Unbeknownst to me, the men in his family had a reputation for being players, womanizers, and abusers. For the first few months that Quintin and I dated I did not see any signs of that. He appeared to be very loyal to me and he was always very sweet and would go out of his way to do nice things for me all of the time.

Slowly I began to see little signs that Quintin was changing. The first thing I noticed is that Quintin was a little jealous and protective of me. Nothing overt in the beginning, in fact I thought it was kind of cute but that wouldn't last long. Soon my instincts began to tell me danger was lurking in the horizon.

It was a warm beautiful sunny day. I was still working at the community center as the peer counselor. All of the girls at the community center were excited because there was a basketball tournament at Penn Park that weekend and guys from Beloit, Milwaukee, and other cities were coming to Madison for the tournament. All of the girls were talking about how fine the boys were from Milwaukee and Beloit. It was going to be a huge event.

I can't lie, I was excited about seeing the fine boys too. I did not want to cheat on Quintin but I was sure going to get my look on. I had to close up the center that day. I went to the back to throw out the trash. I opened the door and Quintin scared the crap out of me.

I said in a shocked high-pitched voice, "Quintin what are you doing back here?" It was something about his demeanor and the look on his face that sent chills through me. I could feel that something was about to happen.

He just looked at me as though he was staring straight through me and yelled, "Where the fuck you goin'?!"

I just stood there in shock. Quintin had never spoke to me that way before. As nervous as I was I got mad and yelled, "Who do you think you are talking to?"

At first, he seemed to calm down because he could tell I was upset and said, "I'm sorry, I shouldn't have talked to you like that." We both calmed down and I told him I was going to the basketball tournament at Penn Park. Just that quick he got angry again and yelled, "When were you going to tell me?!"

That crap pissed me off so bad before I knew it I yelled, "You aren't my daddy, I don't have to tell you where I am or what I'm doing!" In a sudden burst of anger Quintin grabbed me by my shirt and threw me on the ground.

My feelings were hurt more than anything. I fell in some dirt so my clothes got dirty. I got up and ran towards the bus stop. Thank God there was a bus coming. I jumped on the bus and went home. As soon as I walked into my room my phone was ringing. We did not have caller ID back then but somehow, I knew it was Quintin. I did not answer the phone. I had no desire to speak to him ever again. As far as I was concerned it was over point blank! He must have called me at least twenty-five times that night. Eventually, I just took the phone off the hook.

When I heard my parents come in the house that evening I went downstairs to tell them what happened, but when I got down there I froze up and decided not to tell them. I don't know why I didn't tell them because in that moment I hated Quintin and I never wanted to see him again. I just went back upstairs and thought about what happened that day. I knew it was really bad and I should never put up with anyone putting their hands on me.

I stayed away from Quintin for about three or four months, but eventually he wormed his way back in with his apologies, cards, candy, and flowers. Things went well for a while until one day Quintin asked my parents for permission to take me to the movies. My parents said yes and told Quintin I needed to be home by 9:00 that night. Quintin came to pick me up. He did not have a driver's license yet, so his Uncle Gilbert was driving. His uncle had a really nice car. We sat in the back seat and he chauffeured us around.

We headed over to the south side of Madison so his uncle could pick up his girlfriend. Before I knew it, Quintin pulled out a joint and lit it up. I was in shock. I had no idea Quintin smoked marijuana and honestly, I did not know anything about drugs. I asked him not to smoke the joint and to put it away. I told him he should not be using drugs.

After I said it his uncle turned around and said in his country accent, "Mane, you betta' handle that bitch talking to you like that."

Suddenly, Quintin grabbed me by the neck and chocked me until I couldn't breathe. I began to panic and I grabbed his hands to try to pull them off of my neck. I could feel myself blacking out and suddenly he let go of my neck.

I was coughing and crying and trying to catch my breath. I begged his uncle to let me out of the car. I just wanted to go home. Quintin told me to shut the fuck up and sit back. I was afraid so I sat back and did not say anything else. When I got home that night Quintin got out the car with me and started crying. He said he was high and would never hit me under normal circumstances. I hated to see anyone crying so I hugged him and went in the house.

I went upstairs to my bedroom when I got in the house and went straight to the bathroom to look at my neck. I had three red marks on my neck and a large bruise. For the next few days I tried my best to avoid my parents so that they would not notice the bruises on my neck. Somehow, I knew this was not going to stop. I decided that I would just try to see Quintin less and maybe he would just go away but the more I stayed away the more he tracked me down.

As if there wasn't enough going on, I found out in late spring of 1980 that I was pregnant at fifteen years old. Quintin seemed happy about it but I wasn't. My daddy wanted me to get an abortion. He was worried about what kind of future I would have with a baby at sixteen years old and a boyfriend like Quintin.

By that point, my parents were aware of Quintin's abusive patterns and tried their best to get me to leave Quintin alone. Things went from bad to worse after I got pregnant. Now that I was carrying his baby Quintin had this mentality that he owned me and he became even more controlling and abusive.

Quintin had beat the crap out of me several times since that time and to be honest there were so many beatings that I can't remember when they got worse. What I do know is the push turned into choking me and choking me turned into punching me in my face and punching me in the face turned into beating the crap out of me. Quintin kept really long nails so sometimes when he beat me he would scratch up my neck and it would look like a grizzly bear attacked me.

I eventually got tired of Quintin putting his hands on me. If that wasn't bad enough, he started cheating on me often. I had enough of his disrespectful, abusive behavior and made the decision to end our relationship once and for all. I remember the day I did it. I called Quintin and told him that it was over and I never wanted to see him again. I was about 8 months pregnant at that point. Before I knew it Quintin had pulled up to my house and came to the door and asked me to come outside.

I could tell he was mad, but I wasn't scared because I did not think Quintin was crazy enough to hit me in front of my house. At first, he was apologetic and begging me to stay with him, but I told him I was about to have a baby and I did not want my baby around that kind of violence. Quintin became irate and took off with me in the car. We ended up on East Washington Avenue which was about seven or eight miles from my house. Quintin stopped the car and said, "Get out bitch!"

It was dark and I didn't have any bus fare to get home. I told him I needed bus fare, but he wouldn't give it to me. He told me to get out again because he had to get to a party at East High School. I refused to get out because I was eight months pregnant and did not have a way home. Quintin became furious and grabbed me by the neck and started punching me in my face.

My baby was not born yet but my maternal instincts kicked in and I leaned over to the passenger door and used my left foot to kick Quintin in the face. I pulled every ounce of strength I had in me and held his face up against the driver's side door with my foot. Quintin was screaming. I took my other foot and kicked the crap out of his stomach and I tried to kick him in the balls.

Eventually, he took his hands off of me and I grabbed the door and ran out of the car. This cab driver saw me crying and screaming and he gave me a ride home for free. When I got home I told my parents what Quintin did and we called the police and I filed a restraining order against him. Quintin did not bother me again until one day after my daughter LaToya was born.

My beautiful newborn little girl was about two weeks old. She had been running a fever. I called the pediatrician and initially I was instructed to give her some medication to keep her fever down but instead of getting better she got worse. LaToya's fever went up to 103.6 and my mom said we needed to take her to the hospital. I was so upset and crying because I did not understand what happened. She was so happy and healthy just two days ago. I felt like a bad mother because my baby was so sick.

When we got to the ER the doctor did a spinal tap on my daughter. They suspected she had spinal meningitis and the test confirmed it. Things were touch and go for about a day and a half. The doctor gave me a grim report and said if LaToya did pull through she would likely have brain damage.

I never left my baby's side. On the evening of the second day, LaToya's fever broke and she began to improve. The nurse knew I had been there for two days straight so she told me to go home and get a good night's sleep. She promised to call me if LaToya's condition changed. I kissed my little sweetheart and took the bus home.

I had a lot on my mind that night and was feeling overwhelmed. So much had changed in my life in just a few short months. I used to be so strong and confident and now I felt like a weak empty vessel. Every time Quintin punched me it's as though he was chipping away at my inner essence and all that was left was a hollow shell. Now, I was a mother at sixteen years old with no clue about how to raise a child. All I knew was I was going to take care of her and give her the best life that I could. I knew I couldn't depend on Quintin to help me raise her so my education was the tool that would empower me to become successful and raise my daughter. I just wanted to protect her from everything that I had experienced.

It was dark outside and I did not feel like going home yet so I decided to get off the bus at Penn Park so I could think. I sat on the ledge of the wooden jungle gym. I had been sitting at the park for about twenty minutes when I heard this loud pop. Quintin had snooped up behind me while I was sitting there and punched me on the side of my head. I fell back and hit the ground really hard.

I think I was unconscious for a moment because when I came to Quintin was beating me profusely. I felt like I was being attacked by a grizzly bear. He just kept punching me in my face, kicking me in my head, and he grabbed my neck and chocked me until I could no longer breathe. I thought he was going to kill me. All I could think about was my baby LaToya. How would she survive without her mother?

I think a car must have passed the park or something because all of a sudden Quintin took off running. I was in so much pain I couldn't cry or move. Every part of my body ached. I laid there lifeless, I could smell the blood protruding from my mouth and my head. I don't know how long I laid there before I found the energy to get up. The park was about two blocks from my house. The walk home felt like it took me an eternity. I was in tremendous pain and I trembled with every step that I took. I finally made it home and I was trying to scream out so my parents would come outside and get me but they could not hear me.

My parents had given up on the idea that I would ever leave Quintin and even though it was really over I don't think they believed me. There had been countless moments where my daddy went out looking for Quintin after he assaulted me. I was told that one time my daddy went looking for Quintin with a gun. After the last time I reconciled my relationship with Quintin, my parents were done. They were tired and felt like the more they tried to keep me from Quintin the more I ran to him so when I broke up with him the last time they did not believe me.

The flight up the stairs and into my house felt as though I was walking on an escalator that was moving in place. Even though I was victimized by Quintin's abuse I was afraid to walk in the house for fear of my parent's reaction. I slowly opened the door and walked in the house. Our house had a sunken living room so when I walked in my parents were sitting on the couch together watching television. I will never forget the look on their faces as long as I live, but it was their response that shocked me. My parents just stared at me for a moment and then turned right back around a watched television. I could see the shock on their face but immediately following was disappointment.

I just stood there for a moment waiting for them to get up and come clean my wounds but it never happened. After I realized my parents weren't going to help me I went to the bathroom. I was paralyzed in disbelief when I looked in the mirror. I could hardly recognize myself. I had two black eyes, there was blood dripping from my head, a huge knot on my temple, my nose was bleeding, bruises all over my face, I was bleeding from my left ear, and there were scratches on my neck that tore deep into the flesh on my neck like I had been attacked by a lion. I wanted to cry but I was in too much pain. I got a towel and cleaned myself up and called the police.

The police came and took my statement about the incident and gave me a card with the Dane County District Attorney's phone number on it. I didn't sleep well that night because I was in a great deal of pain. When I woke up the next morning my eyes were so swollen they were almost closed. I took a shower and got dressed and took the city bus to the District Attorney's office. I felt so embarrassed when I got on the bus. Everyone was staring at me, almost in disbelief. The District Attorney was a middle aged attractive white man.

When I walked through his door he got up and grabbed me and helped me walk over to the chair. He asked me my name and asked me if I got jumped. I explained the events that took place the night before. He had his assistant come into the office and she took a lot of photos of me. I think the charges were reduced later but he wanted to charge Quintin with attempted murder because of how bad he beat me. Subsequently, Quintin was arrested and served about eight months in jail.

What makes women and young girls stay in abusive relationships? That is a complicated and loaded question but rather than spend a lot of time talking about that I would rather tell you why I feel I left after a year and a half of his abuse. I want to take you back to two critical moments for me.

After I got pregnant I saw my life through a different lens. It was no longer about me it was about my daughter, LaToya. I wanted more for her. It was something about Quintin trying to attack me while I was pregnant that confirmed that he did not care about me or my daughter. I wanted more for her and loved her more than I loved myself and allowed that to be the fuel that ignited my will to want to leave.

This may be shocking to some of you, but the second event that gave me the strength to put an end to Quintin's abuse once and for all was when I came home after the last horrific assault and my parents did not help me. For some reason, when they got involved and talked about Quintin and about what they were going to do to him it's almost as though I became protective of Quintin. When they backed off, I was forced to see him for who he really was. I am grateful to my parents for what they did that day.

After Quintin was arrested and incarcerated, I felt like my life had a new beginning. It was as if I saw grey and now I could see the world in color. My entire outlook on life changed and I was finding my way back to living a happy normal life with my daughter.

Leaving Quintin blessed me with a renewed vision of my self-worth. In the end his manipulation and controlling tactics collapsed right from under him. Quintin was released from jail that next summer. Quintin would soon find out the broken, weak, little girl that he once dated was long gone. One beautiful sunny afternoon my friend Debra and I were walking to a neighborhood party. Just like when we first met, Quintin pulled up on me and Debra on his ten speed bike. You would have thought after everything that happened Quintin would have known to stay away from me. Unlike me, Quintin had not changed at all.

Quintin started cursing at me as he pulled up on me and Debra and yelled, "Where the fuck is my daughter bitch?!" I tried to keep my composure and reminded Quintin that I had a restraining order against him. Before I realized it he jumped off his bike and thrust towards me. In an instant I positioned myself and started beating the crap out of Quintin. It was as though every act of violence and verbal abuse I ever endured came pouring out of me all at once. I think I blacked out because when I came to Quintin was running from me, dragging his bike along with him like a little (you fill in the bleep). By the time Debra and I got to the party half the south side of Madison already heard about it. In the end I got a little sweet revenge of my own and Quintin never put his hands on me ever again.

In the end what I realized was that the only power Quintin ever had on me was the power I submitted to him. There is nothing sweeter than taking back your power from someone who tried to destroy you.

Quintin has been in and out of prison most of his life since that time. I wish him only the best and pray that he finds peace. Quintin apologized, sincerely apologized for the way he treated me after our daughter grew up. I told him I forgave him years ago and then asked him to forgive himself.

The doctor's told me my daughter LaToya may never be able to speak, talk, or walk after she was diagnosed with spinal meningitis but God had other plans. LaToya has grown up to be an absolutely beautiful (both internally and externally), Christian woman and mother. She is married and has given me three of the most incredible, beautiful, creative, intelligent, and gifted grandchildren any grandmother could hope for. I have no regrets. My daughter has made my journey as a mother a beautiful experience and being a grandmother is the icing on the cake.

My relationship and my daughter's relationship with Quintin's mother is very close to this day and there are times I feel Quintin was placed into our lives to give us his mother. Bunchy is one of the most beautiful and amazing women I know and our family is so blessed to have her in our lives. She has been my daughter's spiritual foundation and to this day remains involved in her life.

Sister's Keeper

Our brothers and sisters are there with us from the dawn of our personal stories to the inevitable dusk.
~Susan Scarf Merell

God has a way of blessing us with what we need before we realize we need it. For me that blessing was my brother Pastor Joseph Horne-Edwards. My brother and I shared a special bond from the very beginning and we were equally over protective of one another. In fact, many of my childhood fights were because I was protecting my little brother. My brother loved to pick on me like most siblings do and we had a ton of wonderful memories together as children. I do not personally know of any brother and sister that are as close as me and my brother. My love for my brother runs very deep and there is nothing I would not do or sacrifice for him.

There is one very significant memory that I would like to share with you. When my brother and I were young we were quite a mischievous pair, always getting into something. There were these islands of glass rocks on the property of the apartments where our family lived. I was seven or eight years old at the time and my brother was three or four. The glass rocks were very sharp and could cut you. Some of the children in our apartment complex, my brother, and I included had sustained some pretty bad cuts and injuries from those rocks so my parents warned us not to play in the rocks.

Well, my brother, being the little hard head that he was, did not listen and was playing in the rocks one day. Me, being the protective sister that I am, told my brother to get his behind away from the rocks and of course he did not listen. Somehow, we started arguing with each other and I cannot remember how we got on the subject but the next thing I knew I yelled to my brother, "You are going to grow up and be a preacher one day."

My brother was furious and said, "I'm not going to be no stupid preacher!" and started throwing some of the rocks at me. I just laughed at him as I always did. I don't know how I knew but when my brother and I were children I always knew he was anointed and I didn't even know what being anointed was. God knew that I was going to need a strong spiritual advisor later in my life. My ex-husband was my first one and my brother was my second.

My brother took my mother's death especially hard. Unlike me and my mother, my brother and my mother shared a very special and close bond. My mother was my brother's everything. Shortly after my mother died my brother moved to Washington D.C. with a close family friend and his mother.

That was a very difficult time for both of us. I wanted to take care of my brother but my ex-husband and I were just starting our lives together and we were young with very little resources. My brother lived with us for a little while before he moved to D.C., but it did not last long.

My brother was a bit of a rebel after my mother died. He had a rap group that he and a good friend of his started called the Def Kali. They were fantastic and became local celebrities in Madison. Unfortunately, my brother got involved in drugs and drinking and was headed down the wrong path. I stayed on my brother's behind all the time, especially after my mother died, but like most young people he thought he was invincible and knew everything. My ex-husband took my little brother in as his own and tried to guide him in the right direction but as most young people do, my brother did not heed to our warnings.

I'll never forget the day I found out my brother had traveled to Jamaica and was set up to be the fall guy to try and smuggle some drugs back to America. My brother was arrested, detained and had to serve a year in a Jamaican prison and for those of you that don't know about Jamaican prisons, some men do not live through the experience. As you can imagine, after losing my mother already this experience felt much like a bereavement to me. I felt so helpless because there was nothing I could do to help my brother.

I was very strong in my faith during that period in my life and my relationship with God was my fortress. I wrote my brother often to try to encourage him to never give up. We were not sure at that time how long my brother was going to be in prison but he was facing a very long sentence. I prayed and fasted for my brother often. As difficult as things were and as bad as things looked, I kept my faith that God would intervene.

One day I had a dream or a vision. It felt so real that I cried when I came to. I distinctly saw, as though it was happening in 3D, two visions of my brother. One vision was of my brother in a coffin coming off of an airplane and the other was a vision of my brother preaching in front of multitudes of people. I was frightened by the vision but somehow, I knew this was a message from God and that God wanted me to write my brother and tell him that he was about to get a second chance in life and that his choices would determine his outcome.

I wrote my brother and told him that he was anointed and destined for greatness and that God was going to use him as a vessel to bring multitudes to Christ. I told him he needed to surrender his life to Christ and that I needed him to survive. When my brother wrote me back it was the first time he embraced the vision I had always seen of him becoming a preacher.

God intervened on my brother's behalf and he was released from the Jamaican prison after serving a year's time. My brother made a decision while he was in prison that he would eventually commit his life to Christ and when he did he was going to be serious about it. Eight years after my brother came back home he was saved and committed his life to Christ. My brother was eventually ordained as an elder and is now a preacher. He has a beautiful wife and two beautiful daughters and has been the perfect example of the type of man I want in my own life. My brother and his wife have the most beautiful marriage I have ever witnessed and it gives me hope that I too can have that someday.

As I have expressed in my book, I had many difficult moments in my life, more than I can write about and because I was not raised in the church I did not have a strong spiritual foundation until later in life. I committed my life to Christ after I met my ex-husband. It was my ex-husband who brought me into the Christian faith through a church revival. God then used me to bring my brother to Him and now my brother is my greatest spiritual advisor. It amazes me that as I child I could see God's plan. When His plan manifested, God used my brother to pull me out of some of the most difficult and dark moments in my life, especially my divorce. I would not have made it without him. I began to lose faith during my divorce and strayed away from the path God chose for my life and my children's lives. My brother is one of the people that were instrumental in pulling me back in. I would have never made it without his love and guidance.

God knew what I needed when He formed me in the womb and when He hand designed my brother, He formed him with purpose. I was a part of that purpose. God knew I would need my brother when I entered the valley and more than thirty years before I needed it God had already worked things out.

Divine Intervention

For I know the plans I have for you, declares the Lord, plans to prosper you and not to harm you, plans to give you hope and a future. Jeremiah 29:11 NIV

~God

My marriage had many periods of up and downs. My husband and I were married young and often saw things much differently. It was December of 1993. My ex-husband and I were having our share of problems in our marriage at the time and I was pregnant with our youngest daughter LaShawna. Because we had our daycare and were self-employed we did not have any health insurance. When I got pregnant I was eligible for health insurance through the State of Wisconsin for me and my children. I could have never imagined at the time how tremendous a blessing that would be in the upcoming months.

My daughter LaNisha was 4 years old. She was very bright and intelligent, but she also had a mean streak in her a mile long. She was hilarious because she had such a bad temper that when she was 2 years old she made up a curse word, "burner shurners." Whenever she said that word we knew someone in the house was getting cursed out. From birth LaNisha was always extremely bright. LaNisha loved learning and loved to read.

The date was December 18th, 1993. LaNisha was four years old at the time. She started showing symptoms of the flu. Initially, it did not seem bad but soon I would see that our daughter was gravely ill. One morning I went into LaNisha's room to wake her up for school. She was pale and lethargic. I called my ex-husband and told him our daughter was sick and that I was taking her to the doctor. LaNisha seemed to be losing weight, but I had no idea how much until I tried to put her underwear on her and they fell back down. My heart sunk in that moment, because I knew something was terribly wrong. Our daughter had lost a lot of weight in just a few short days.

Normally, whenever I did anything I prayed but in my panic I rushed my daughter to the ER without praying. My ex-husband did not come with me the first day I took LaNisha to the hospital and it was a good thing he didn't. The nurse was very rude and yelled and told me to put my daughter down and to stop spoiling her. LaNisha was very weak and could not walk so I obviously did not listen to her. I don't know what was going on that day but all I can say is Satan was busy. It took the doctor forever to come in and see LaNisha and when he did I can remember seeing his blood shot red eyes. It looked as though he had not slept all night. I was very disturbed by it. He was short with me when asking questions and showed little concern for my baby. After he examined my daughter, he told me she had the flu and told me to take her home and give her some Pedialyte for her dehydration.

I was extremely irritated because I knew that whatever was going on it was serious. That evening when my ex-husband came home from work he took one look at my daughter and he knew that whatever was going on with her was much worse than the flu. My ex-husband had been studying the bible and he remembered seeing a verse in the bible that talked about hyssop tea being a healing tea. He went out and bought the tea and we gave LaNisha some of the tea and prayed over her.

A few hours later, sometime after midnight, LaNisha threw up blood and we rushed LaNisha back to the ER. The date was December 19th. This time we remembered to pray first. When we arrived at the ER the nursing staff was very attentive and kind. They told me and my ex-husband that our daughter was extremely sick and took a lot of test. We knew it was bad because they would not allow us in the exam room with her. The doctor told us LaNisha was gravely ill and they would not be able to diagnose her until the test results were in. I went out to a waiting area in the back of the ER and my ex-husband went to the phone booth to call his mother. I sat there numb and lifeless. What was happening? I was hurt and broken. I just remember feeling and knowing that I needed to pray, but I was numb and couldn't move.

As I was sitting there this Caucasian man in a wheelchair came up to me. He placed his hand on my hand and tried to comfort me. He asked me if that was my little girl in the ER. I remember his hand feeling so warm and soothing. At first, I did not even look up at him and I just said, "Yes, she is." He told me not to be afraid and asked me if he could pray with me. At that point, I looked up and told him yes. When I looked in this young man's eyes I was stunned at how beautiful they were. His eyes were crystal clear like diamonds with no color.

The young man took my hands and began to pray. Before I knew it, he was speaking in tongues. I need you to understand that I was a huge skeptic of speaking in tongues because normally all it sounded like to me was a bunch of meaningless jibber jabber and everyone that did it sounded the same to me. But this was different. This young man's voice resonated like beautiful music and it sounded like a real language. I was filled with emotion and it was as though the Holy Spirit took over my body. Suddenly, I felt comfort. When the young man finished praying he hugged me and told me our baby was going to be alright and then disappeared around the corner. I was still in a little bit of shock about everything that was happening.

My ex-husband came back from calling his mother. I told him about the young man in the wheelchair and we went to go find him to thank him. We did not see him anywhere so we began to ask the ER staff if they had seen him. They told us there had not been anyone in the ER that day in a wheelchair and kept asking me if I was sure he was in a wheelchair. I told them he was definitely in a wheelchair and they insisted once again that no one came to the ER that day in a wheelchair.

We stood there confused. Suddenly the doctor came up to us and told us the test results were in and our daughter's blood glucose level was over 700 mg/dl, 70 mg/dl was normal. I did not know anything about diabetes at the time so I did not know what that meant. The doctor explained that LaNisha had diabetes and she needed to be rushed by ambulance to Children's Hospital.

My ex-husband would not allow our daughter to go to the hospital by ambulance. He wanted us to be with her if something were to happen, so we rushed her to Children's Hospital. The trip to Children's was normally about a twenty-five to thirty minute trip and my ex-husband got her there in about seven minutes.

My ex-husband and I were in separate vehicles, but I prayed the entire time I traveled to Children's hospital. When I looked my baby in the eyes before we left the hospital I could see that she was on death's door. She was barely breathing and she was moaning the entire time. When we pulled up to Children's ER there was a team of eight doctors and nurses standing at the door that grabbed LaNisha from my ex-husband's arms and rushed off with her.

At that moment, it became real to my ex-husband and I about just how sick LaNisha was. My husband went to call his mother and some of our family. The doctors came out and told us that LaNisha had Type I Juvenile Diabetes. She was in a state called ketoacidosis and had slipped into a coma. He told us the next few hours were critical. I asked the doctor if my baby was going to live. He told me they could not answer that question. I stood there in shock. I could not believe what I was hearing. I became consumed with feelings of fear, anxiety, confusion, and helplessness all at once.

LaNisha was moved to the ICU. It is very difficult for me to describe everything I was feeling in that moment. I just remember feeling very numb and helpless because there was nothing I could do to help my baby. I stood there and watched my baby's lifeless body in the ICU. They did not have any chairs in the room where she was. When the nurse told me that my ex-husband and I could not stay overnight in the room with her, I broke down. I begged her to let me lay on the floor next to my baby. If she died I did not want her to be alone. I wanted her to know her mommy was right there.

The hospital floor was cold and hard but it did not bother me at all, I just wanted to be near my baby. The ICU nurses were worried about me lying on the floor because I was seven months pregnant at the time. As I laid on the hospital floor that first night I was crying and asking God why he was allowing this to happen to my child. I don't know if I was angry with God, but for the first time since my mother died I questioned His plan. My ex-husband went home to take care of our other two daughters and get them off to school. I don't think I stopped praying once that whole night.

It was real touch and go for the first few days but after the second night we began to see signs of improvement. On the fourth day, God showed up and showed out and LaNisha's condition improved dramatically. I stayed in the hospital with her the entire week to learn how to take care of her. My ex-husband stayed as much as he could and would go back and forth from the hospital and home to take care of our other children. Our family had been praying that LaNisha would be released from the hospital by Christmas Eve and our prayers were answered. Our baby came home December 24th and it was the most memorable Christmas our family ever had.

I often thought back to that day in the ER and thought about the man in the wheelchair. Somehow in our hearts my ex-husband and I knew that God sent an angel in the flesh to save our daughter. The events that took place that day were a miracle and I knew it. The day LaNisha was discharged from the hospital after she got sick we went down to the ER to thank the doctor that saved her.

I will never forget the look on his face when LaNisha and I came around the corner. He looked like he saw a ghost. Although he did not tell us, that doctor thought LaNisha was going to die the day she arrived in the ER. He was so thrilled to see her and he gave her the biggest hug. I could even see that he was a little emotional. He gave LaNisha a little frog off of his jacket. LaNisha loved that little frog and we still have it to this day.

Later that next spring, I got my confirmation that God had indeed sent an angel to save LaNisha. The children from my daycare and I were sitting in our circle having worship as we did every morning. It was always one of my favorite times of the day. That morning our devotion was about angels. As we began to discuss angels I told the children that they all had a guardian angel. LaNisha raised her hand and kept it up anxiously begging me to pick her so that she could tell us something. I let LaNisha tell her story and what she said that day has deepened my faith in ways that I could have never imagined.

LaNisha described feeling very sick in the ER that day and remembering an angel coming into her room. She said, "Mommy my angel came and he flew over me as I was lying there and he spread his wings wide open like this (spreading out her arms) and there was a pretty blue light that was warm. My angel wrapped his arms around me and then I felt better mommy."

The tears started pouring down my face and I grabbed my baby and held her. I could not stop crying. I knew in that moment that God kept his covenant with me where he promised in his word that he would never put more on us than we can bear and losing my child could have literally taken me out of here. I was so humbled in that moment to know that God loved us so much that he sent an angel to come in the flesh on His behalf to save our precious beautiful daughter.

In that moment, I received confirmation of what I already knew in my heart to be true and that was that LaNisha had a divine calling on her life and God was not going to allow *ANYTHING* to interfere.

God interceded in many ways during that time because my ex-husband and I had been having a lot of marital problems and that all changed the instant LaNisha got sick. The days, weeks, and months following LaNisha's illness were rough, but together we managed and learned to care for her. LaNisha was always strong and never complained. I admired her so much for her strength and positive outlook on life. She was only four years old and she handled her circumstances like a champion. LaNisha never complained for years and I drew my strength from her.

If I had not been pregnant with my daughter LaShawna when LaNisha got sick the hospital bills would have wiped our family out financially. Because I was pregnant at the time, I was eligible for short term health insurance. There is no doubt in my mind that God intervened on our behalf. Me and my ex-husband's preschool prospered after that and we built a beautiful home in Germantown, Wisconsin to raise our children.

About four years later when LaNisha was eight years old, I was sitting on my bed reading when LaNisha came to my room and walked up to me and collapsed on my lap. She was distraught and said, "Mommy I am tired of having diabetes, why did God do this to me?"

I could see how upset my baby was and it was the first time that I saw her spirit broken. Just as I had always drawn strength from her I knew that this time I had to be her strength. I was honest and explained to LaNisha that I did not know why God allowed this to happen to her. I told her that I was sure that God had a much bigger plan for her life than we did and in the end, she would understand why. I told her God was going to use her diabetes to help change the world. I told LaNisha we could not lose faith and we had to trust God no matter how difficult things seem. She hugged me and we prayed together and she was back to her joyful self in no time.

When I tell you God was quick and expeditious in His response, you cannot even begin to imagine. About a week after LaNisha and I prayed for answers that day in my room I received a letter in the mail. The letter was from the Juvenile Diabetes Research Foundation. The letter stated that they were preparing to hold their first annual Children's Congress in Washington D.C. that year and they were looking to choose two delegates to send to Washington D.C. from each state.

When I read the letter, tears poured down my face. I was sitting in my room audibly praising God. In that moment, I *knew* LaNisha was going to be one of the delegates. I was so excited I swear I felt like I could faint from the joy I felt in that moment. When LaNisha got home from school we read the letter together again and the look on my baby's face when she read that letter was all the comfort I needed to affirm everything our family had been through since LaNisha got sick.

That afternoon LaNisha sat down and wrote her letter. I did not have to help her much. LaNisha was a straight A student. After we sealed the envelope we prayed over the letter and mailed it. It did not take long for JDRF to respond. I stood in the foyer of our home while my ex-husband and I opened the letter. She did it! We grabbed each other and jumped around like two crazy people. Oh the joy I felt in that moment was like no joy I had ever felt. I was crying, screaming, and praising God all at the same time.

I grabbed the letter and rushed off to LaNisha's school to let her read it. She was so happy and excited that she cried. I can't properly express in words the joy I felt when my baby grabbed me and said, "God does love me mommy, he does!"

Wait, it gets better. The letter informed us that of the one hundred delegates chosen for the Children's Congress, four would be chosen to do a testimony before the Senate Appropriations Committee. Our State Senator Herb Kohl sat on the committee. You guessed it, a couple of weeks later we were notified that LaNisha was one of the four children out of one hundred delegates chosen to speak to the Senate Appropriations Committee.

Soon we were off to Washington D.C. LaNisha was treated like a celebrity when we arrived. It was so exciting. During LaNisha's speech she commissioned congress to allocate more funding for research for juvenile diabetes. She promised the members of the committee that if they did not find a cure she was going to grow up and become a medical researcher and find a cure herself. LaNisha did so well during her speech that Senator Kohl asked LaNisha to do the opening speech at Wisconsin's State Democratic National Convention later that year.

LaNisha was chosen to attend the Children's Congress again the next year to be one of about eight children chosen to speak with some of the top scientist from the National Institute of Health about stem cell research. LaNisha went on to graduate valedictorian of both her middle and high school class. LaNisha was awarded the Bill Gates Millennium scholarship and has gone on to receive her Bachelor's degree in biological sciences, her Master's degree in biology and she is currently a graduate student at the University of Texas Medical Branch studying cell biology preparing for her qualification exam for her doctoral studies next spring.

My daughter kept the promise that she made to the Senate Appropriations Committee that day and is well on her way to becoming a medical researcher and I fully anticipate that my baby will one day be the recipient of the Nobel Peace Prize. Our family endured the valley together through that experience. In hind sight, it gave me a greater appreciation for embracing adversity and it reminds me to have faith in God's purpose and calling for our lives no matter how grim things may appear.

The period of my life when my daughter was first diagnosed with diabetes was almost as difficult as losing my mother. God knew what I needed and He restored our family and our faith through an experience that during that time felt as though God had abandoned us. No matter how horrible things seem don't lose your faith in God.

When LaNisha graduated from high school I had already lost everything. I did not have the funds or resources to pay for her college education. Without the Bill Gates Millennium Scholarship LaNisha's aspiration to become a medical researcher may have never come to fruition. I began to realize that when God has designed something for your life He will provide every resource necessary to make it happen. To this day it breaks my heart that LaNisha did not get a brand new car like her two older sisters when she graduated as valedictorian of her high school, she certainly deserved it but I poured my soul into blessing her with a memorable celebration. In spite of the fact that she did not get her car, she remained true to her humble character and never complained and was so grateful.

As God says in I Corinthians 14:33, "God is not the author of confusion." Everything God does has purpose and order and is for the good. God took what Satan intended to use to take my daughter's life to propel her into greatness far beyond anything we could have ever foreseen.

Storage Space

Sometimes God brings transition to create transformation.

~Lynn Cowell

So, there I was, standing in front of a 10' x 25' storage space. My entire life stored inside a space made of metal and steel. How did my life come to this? It was May 14, 2011. It was very difficult in that moment for me and my children to comprehend just how much our lives had changed in a few short months from a circumstance that propelled out of control a few years ago. There I was with 32 cents in my pocket and a plane ticket to Atlanta. No plan and no money, just the empty remnants of a dream deferred.

There is no way I can reconstruct how I arrived at this point without exposing experiences in my life that I refuse to divulge, but I will take you back to the day it all accelerated out of control. I owned and operated my Christian state licensed preschool for over twenty-six years and it was all about to come plummeting down. It was a progression of events that started after I filed for a divorce from my husband in 1999. Trying to juggle the alimony payments I had to pay my husband and the expansion of my preschool took a financial toll on my business. Wisconsin is a community property, no fault divorce state so because my ex-husband was trying to start a new business and was not working any other job at the time that I filed for my divorce I had to pay him alimony.

During my divorce from my ex-husband, I became consumed with proving to him that I would not only survive without him, but that I would excel, do better, and become stronger without him. At the time, I made some very poor executive decisions regarding the expansion of my preschool and as a result I lost my home, my vehicles, filed for bankruptcy, fell behind in my taxes, all while paying my ex-husband what started out as $3000 per month in alimony and was later reduced to $2000 per month in alimony payments. I was also caring for my beautiful daughter who was diagnosed with Type I Juvenile Diabetes with no health insurance.

I was determined to prove to my ex-husband that he could not and would not break me. I was so at peace with my decision to leave my ex-husband that I fooled myself into believing that I was not wounded nor broken when I left him. I knew my worth and even after four children and sixteen years of marriage I was not going to tolerate infidelity, especially in the manner that it happened in my marriage.

It all started with collection letters and tax levies against my business, often without warning, leaving me to find solutions for the financial devastation it caused my business, at times even struggling to figure out how I was going to pay my staff and pay my business expenses. Generally, the solution came with strategies that included not paying myself to ensure my staff and my preschool were taken care of. I was fully cognizant of the notion that if I did not take care of my business it would not take care of me, which was short for, *at times I would come last.*

After a couple of failed payment plans with the State of Wisconsin Department of Revenue and my oldest daughter's move to Texas I lost my passion to fight for my business. I promoted my daughter LaToya to director of my preschool. Her passion to support my vision for my preschool was the only thing that kept me fighting and after she left I no longer had the will to keep my preschool open.

With all of the state budget cuts and the aftermath of the State of Wisconsin's W-2 initiative, it was becoming more difficult to find child care teachers that were both passionate and qualified to teach children at the level that I expected for my program. Educating these beautiful minds is what I lived for. I had become so consumed with operating a program that fostered excellence that it became who I was and no longer what I do.

While for some of you that may not appear to be negative, it is critical that all of us no matter what we do, have balance in our lives. If we focus too much on one thing, the intangible components of our lives such as family, having a social life, and pursuing other dreams and aspirations wilt away like a plant that has not been watered.

During that time, I was two semesters from completing my Bachelor's degree at the University of Wisconsin's School of Education where I majored in Education Policy and Community Studies/ Community Engagement. Prior to going back to school, I had devoted so much of my adult life to educating my own children and educating the children in my community that between operating my business, being a single mother, sitting on all of the various board of directors I was on, my involvement in my church, and attending all of the sports and other activities my daughters were involved in that it left very little time for me to pursue my education. As my children grew older and started leaving the nest I pursued my passion to further my own education.

This was a fulfilling but challenging time in my life because for the first time since I could remember I was actually doing something for myself and honestly, it just did not feel right. In many ways, it felt selfish and I struggled with it but in all of the calamity and drama evolved around my divorce, it was exactly what I needed to gift me with the peace and serenity I needed to survive such tumultuous times.

I woke up one day and knew it was time to let go of my preschool. Although, it was a very difficult decision for me, it felt right. I knew God had something bigger planned for my life and I also knew that my time in Milwaukee had come to an end so I liquidated all of my assets in my preschool and lived off the earnings until I ran out of money. With no degree, I knew entering the workforce and securing a job that would pay a decent enough salary to care for my daughters would be a challenge.

I think I was in denial of just how bad things were for me. When my truck was repossessed *again* that did not bother me, I had been through that and bounced back before so for me this was familiar territory. As strange as it sounds the day everything hit me was the morning I woke up and my cell phone was off and I had no money to turn it back on. It's something about our connection to the outside world getting cut off that is an instant game changer in how we navigate our way through our day to day.

I lived in a suburb of Milwaukee called Oak Creek, Wisconsin. There were no buses and the only other person I knew that lived out that far was my pastor and his family who became a literal lifeline to me. In fact, I owe my Bachelor's degree to my pastor Eric Bell. He woke up every morning after my truck was repossessed and took me and my daughter to school and campus every day for the remainder of the semester.

My pastor and his family are truly one of my life's greatest blessings. They helped me and my daughter so much during that time. My ex-husband would also pick us up and drop us off at times and I am grateful to him for his support during that period in my life.

After I discovered my cell phone was not on and I had no way of communicating with anyone I think I had a mild anxiety attack. I remember sitting on my couch confused and afraid. I was shaking, my chest felt heavy as though someone was lying on it, I felt as though I couldn't breathe, and my heart felt as though it was beating a thousand beats per second.

I sat there asking myself "How the hell did I get here?" I was numb for about an hour. When I came back to my senses I knew I had to implement a survival strategy. I had about $32 on me at the time and under $100 in my bank account but my cell phone bill was over $200. The one thing I knew is with me living so far removed from everything and everyone, a cell phone was a necessity so I got dressed to go the gas station that was about a half mile from where I lived to buy a Trac prepaid cell phone.

I think I was still in panic mode because I remember hearing and feeling my heart beating so hard it felt as though it would burst through my chest. It was strange because when I walked outside the door of my apartment, I took off running at high speed and then my speed accelerated until I felt as if I were running at the speed of a cheetah. I don't remember ever feeling tired. I think my fear put me in a place where I was operating on full adrenaline.

When I arrived back to my apartment it all hit me at once. As soon as I walked up the stairs in my apartment, I collapsed on my living room carpet and fell and screamed at the top of my lungs. The sound that came out of me was this terrifying wail that exploded from deep in my stomach as if my soul was trying to escape from my body. I lied there lifeless for what appeared to be an eternity.

I just remember thinking, "How am I going to take care of my babies?" Although, my youngest daughter was the only one still living at home I prided myself in always being able to help my children no matter what they needed, especially finances. I did not like seeing my children suffer or needing anything. There is no greater feeling of helplessness than knowing your children are struggling and need you and you are not in a position to help them. I felt so low in that moment that the ideal of dying felt welcoming. I just wanted the pain to stop.

I called my daughter LaTina who lived in Atlanta later that evening. I was careful not to alarm her, I did not want her to know just how bad things were. I remember hearing her sweet voice when she answered the phone. I immediately felt comfort when she answered the phone saying, "Hey mom, how are you feeling?" I think she knew something was wrong but instead of asking me, knowing how proud I was she just said, "It's funny you called because I was just thinking I should call you and talk you into coming down here." She said, "Mom I think God wants you to come here."

LaTina was very protective of me, much in the same manner a son protects his mother and she just wanted her mommy to be alright. I told her I thought she was right and I promised I would look into some flights later that night. After I got off the phone with my daughter I called the bank and I had exactly $74.46 in my bank account. This was mid-March 2010. I called my daughter back and asked her to look at some one-way flights to Atlanta. *Now keep in mind this was March.*

My daughter asked me when I was planning on coming. I told my daughter to look at flights leaving around mid-May. I told her my budget was around $70. She said she found a flight leaving on May 14th for $71.00. I gave her my debit card information and we booked the flight. I want you to pay attention to the timeline for what I am about to tell you next.

On April 11th, I received an eviction notice on my door. I had been living in my apartments for 10 years and up until recently had been a model tenant. I was honest with the leasing office about my circumstances so when I did not pay rent in March they worked with me but when I could not pay April's rent they had to take action. I was scheduled to be in court about three weeks later. I knew that if I did not go to court the sheriff could come and move me out immediately so I made sure I went to the court hearing for the eviction.

During this entire eviction process I began to feel alone, abandoned and unloved by God. I couldn't understand why all of this was happening to me. At my court hearing when my name was called I walked up to the front of the courtroom and after telling the judge I did not have the money to pay my rent I was told if I do not move out of the property by *May 14th* the sheriff would come and move my things out of the property. I stood there stunned, I could not move and I felt as though I was going to faint. That date just kept reverberating through my mind. I stood there speechless and numb thinking, Oh my God!!!! That is the date that my flight leaves for Atlanta, a ticket I bought two months ago.

I remember turning around feeling like everyone in the court room was staring at me and feeling as though the walls of the courtroom were closing in on me. I rushed out of the courtroom looking around trying to find the exit. As I ran outside the tears poured down my face like an endless fountain. For the first time in longer than I could remember I felt God's love and His presence as if He picked me up, cradled me in His arms, and comforted me. Tears are running down my face as I am typing this because to this day that moment still gives me chills. It was in that moment when the judge said that date, *May 14th*, that I knew this was a God thing and so much bigger than me. It's as if he took every tear, every burden, and every heartache from me and left them on the floor of that courtroom. I still did not understand what was happening or what I was going to do but what I did have was the comfort of knowing God was with me.

Entering the Valley

I've changed. Irrevocably. Permanently. My soul is richer and my heart is fuller in brokenness than it ever was without. I've learned true despair, and it's made me learn to appreciate true joy.

~Lexi Behrndt

The day had come, moving day May 13th, 2011. I had spent the past few weeks preparing myself for that day so I was mentally prepared to do what needed to get done so that I could begin my new life in Atlanta. I fell asleep the night before with so many feelings of uncertainty but my greatest anxiety was following through with my decision to leave my youngest daughter LaShawna in Wisconsin with her father. It was LaShawna's senior year in high school and I had struggled back and forth many times about leaving her. Her senior year was such a critical year for her and *nothing* about my decision to leave her felt right, *nothing*.

I spent so many restless nights trying to persuade myself into taking her but my daughter LaTina was already taking on the burden of caring for me until I got back on my feet, how could I ask her to also take care of her little sister. My daughter

LaShawna had been doing pretty well in school for the most part. She had the support of her father, her paternal grandmother and my second youngest daughter LaNisha not to mention our entire family living in Wisconsin as a strong support network for her. I felt I was too unstable and unsure of my future to risk LaShawna's stability and future.

I was supposed to be getting some money to move that morning but it fell through. So, there I was sitting on the edge of my bed, no money for a moving truck, no money to pay for the storage, and no money to take the shuttle to Chicago to board my flight to Atlanta the next morning. I suddenly began to question whether or not this really was a God thing or was it just echoes of hope I fed myself in order to survive the trauma of leaving everyone and everything I knew behind.

I struggled with the decision to call my pastor and ask him for help. Pastor Bell and his wife had already extended so much help to me and it just did not feel right asking him for any help, but I knew I had to do something. I conjured up the courage to call my pastor and I explained everything to him. Like always he was so kind and immediately offered to pay for my moving truck. As tears flowed down my face, I thanked him. I went to pick up the truck and went home to finish packing. My daddy, my brother, my sister-in-law, my daughter LaNisha and her friends and of course my baby girl LaShawna were all there to help me pack everything up. I still did not have the money for the storage space but I also did not have the luxury of putting everything on hold while I figured it out

There I was packing up the last sixteen years of my life inside boxes and bags. It was difficult because I had already lost some of my most treasured and precious possessions in the storage unit I rented when I moved into my apartment because I could not keep up the payments. Just a few shorts months before that day the storage company sold away some of my most precious memories which included videos of our family, photos of my children, and other precious memories to someone who probably just threw them away. It's amazing how something so incredibly precious and valuable to one person can be meaningless to someone else.

Because of that, I found myself apprehensive about letting go of anything and it took forever to pack everything up because I wanted to look over every single item in my apartment and only get rid of the things that were of no importance to me.

We were running out of time. We had the truck packed up with the first load of items that had to go into storage. We had been in such a grind to pack everything up that I had forgotten that I still did not have the money for my storage space. At that time, my daddy was living on his retirement and Social Security payments and he did not have any money to help me and my brother had recently bought a home and funds were still tight for him and his wife. I had to be at the airport in Chicago by 7:00 am which meant I had to be at Mitchell Airport by 4:50 am to catch the first airport shuttle to Chicago.

There was only one person in that moment that I thought could help me. It was someone very special to me. His name is Michael and he had no idea how much my life had changed since he moved to Texas a couple of years before. Just as I knew he would, Michael asked me for the phone number to the storage facility and immediately called and paid for my storage for two months.

We rushed and packed everything into the storage and went back to my apartment to pack up the last of the items. Time went by so fast, I looked up and it was almost 2:00 a.m. and I still had to clean the apartment. It was time for everyone to leave. As I looked into my daddy's eyes before I hugged him goodbye I could see the worry in his face. He held me as if he wanted to protect me from everything that was happening to me and I could feel my daddy's helplessness as he held me.

My daddy is aware that everyone has their breaking point and he knew my children were my lifeline. My daddy admitted to me a few months later that he was afraid to leave me that night because he thought I may try to take my life. He knew how incredibly difficult it was for me to leave my daughters behind.

I tried my best to camouflage my pain and be strong for my family, especially my children. I remember holding my daughters and fighting to maintain my composure so they would not feel me trembling or feel the anguish inside of me. I looked my daughter's in the eyes and reassured them that this was only temporary and that everything was going to be okay. I wasn't sure if I actually believed it myself but I had to be strong for both of them.

I did not realize until everyone was gone that I never got the $30 for my shuttle to Milwaukee. I felt such anguish and defeat in that moment. I remember feeling frustrated, audibly saying to God, "Really God? You are going to allow me to get this far and then let me miss my flight?!"

So, there I was, it was 2:30 in the morning, the shuttle to Chicago O'hare was leaving in two hours and no money to get there. I was not about to call anyone and ask them to get out of bed at 2:30 in the morning and drive all the way to Oak Creek to help me.

I sat there in the middle of the empty apartment ready to give up and suddenly I remembered someone very special to me who was probably the only person that I could think of that would be up that early in the morning. I called him and he answered the phone immediately, very happy to hear from me. Pure had not spoken to me in quite a while and last he knew I was doing quite well in life. He hated to see me in that situation and told me he would come and bring the money for the shuttle and take me to the airport. Pure gave me enough money to get on the shuttle and to buy something to eat when I got to the airport.

I was so grateful to God for the love he showed me that day and for the way he came through for me under such impossible circumstances. I was so secure in those moments and felt God's unfailing love for me. I had been in such a grind in the days leading up to my move that I hadn't been eating or sleeping enough. I don't think it hit me until I got on the bus just how much I had experienced.

So, there I was, a woman that had been successful, educated, and well respected in her community; broke, no plan, no money, and no resources to start over. I remember when I sat down on the bus as it pulled off from the airport it all became so real to me. I was shaking profusely. The tears began to flow and I felt as though I wanted to die.

I remember wanting to scream and fighting to hold it all in in fear that others would hear me. All I could think about was my daughters. How could I leave them? LaNisha lived in the dorms on Marquette University's campus but she was a Type I diabetic and I was always there when she needed me. LaShawna was going to begin her senior year in the fall. I knew how much she needed me and how much my influence would impact her life and there I was leaving them. I hated myself and felt lower than I had ever felt in my life.

As the bus pulled up to O'hare, I walked off the bus slowly. It was cloudy and drizzling that morning. It almost felt like God was crying with me. It was as if everything was moving in slow motion. I remember feeling exhausted. I made it. Soon I would be on my flight to Atlanta to start my life over. I checked my luggage in and that moment it hit me just how emotionally, mentally, and physically drained I was. I felt as though my legs were going to buckle right from under me. There I was walking through the airport, tears flowing, feeling as though I could no longer go on.

I finally made it to the escalator and that's when everything I had experienced in the months leading up to that moment came pouring out of me. I stepped on the escalator and I almost fainted. A gentleman behind me caught me and helped me. He could see that I was crying and he just held me up until we reached the top of the escalator. All of the brokenness, despair, and hopelessness came pouring out of me and I collapsed under it all. He asked me if I needed him to call for help. I told him I just needed to sit down. He walked me over to a bench and helped me sit down. I assured him that I was fine but the look in his eyes told me that he knew that I wasn't and he graciously walked away.

When I boarded the plane, I remember looking out the window during our departure. I could see the drizzle from the rain hitting the window. The sound of the rain lulled me to sleep. God nurtured me through one of the darkest moments in my life and held on to His promise that He would never leave me nor forsake me.

Atlanta

*Do not judge, you do not know what storm I have
asked her to walk through.*
~God

I woke up to the sound of the stewardess' voice instructing us to lift up our seats and prepare for our decent into Atlanta. I had a window seat on the flight and I remembered looking out the window. The sky was so clear and blue and the sun was shining. It was such a contrast from the weather in Chicago when I left earlier that day. As I walked off the plane and through the airport I was so filled with anticipation at the thought of seeing my daughter LaTina.

I walked towards the baggage claim and there she was. I could see those beautiful adorable fat cheeks the moment I laid eyes on her. She looked so beautiful, angelic almost. She grabbed me and hugged me for what seemed like an eternity, as though she wanted to protect me from everything that happened. I needed her and I felt that she needed me.

I was so tickled when we arrived at her house. Her and her partner leased a home in Canton, Georgia which was about forty miles outside of Atlanta. The home was a two-story, cape-cod style, four bedroom home. I felt so loved in that moment because I knew my daughter leased that home just for me. There was no way they needed that much house. They had lived in a one bedroom apartment before I moved there and I could tell that my daughter wanted me to feel comfortable and at home. She even chose a community that was similar to the community we built our home in back in Wisconsin.

I had my own bedroom and I think my baby's intention was for me to stay with her long term and save up as much money as possible to get back on my feet. After she gave me a tour of her home she ran me a hot bath and cooked for me. I remember being so impressed. I didn't even know my daughter could cook. The food was delicious. I think my daughter could tell I still wasn't okay even though I tried to hide behind my smile.

I think my body began to go into shock after I ate. I remember getting into my daughter's jacuzzi tub and falling asleep in the tub. My daughter came and got me out of the tub and helped me back to my bedroom. I slept for three days straight. In those few moments of waking up all I could do was cry. It's almost as though I did not want to wake up. I just wanted to sleep the pain away. I just laid there staring off into space. I could feel the pain deep into the pit of my stomach. I had no appetite. I would just lay there lifeless.

On the third day, I think my daughter began to worry and she was determined to get me out of bed. My baby prayed over me and nursed me back to life. She encouraged me to start getting out and walking, working out, seeking employment, and writing again because she knew I loved to write. It was summer so I wouldn't have classes again until the fall. I slowly came back to life. I got into a routine and started planning my future. I slowly began to forgive myself for leaving my babies and started to believe in myself again. It was a daily struggle but I was doing it.

My plan was to use my school money when I started my classes in the fall to get an apartment in Atlanta. My daughter was not happy about me moving out so soon, but she knew how independent her mom was and she respected it. I did not have transportation so moving in an area that had public transportation was critical to my survival. I found an apartment in the Camp Creek community a few miles from the airport. It was a beautiful community and my apartment was beautiful. It was perfect for me because it not only had a bus route but I could transport from the bus to the trains to get around.

I could not afford cable or internet. I also did not have a cell phone. I managed to get by with just a landline phone in my apartment. I was hired by the State of Georgia and worked in Norcross which was a two to two and a half hour route to work one way so I spent four to five hours daily traveling to and from work on the bus and train. I had to wake up at 4:15 a.m.

every morning and would not get home until about 7:45 p.m. every evening. I had begun classes that fall so I would still have to study when I arrived home, sometimes until 3:00 a.m. and have to start all over again at 4:15 a.m. with only about an hour's sleep.

I was finishing my bachelor's program at the University of Wisconsin-Milwaukee online so it was very difficult for me to function in my classes without any internet. I did what I had to do to get by which included getting off the bus about a little over a half mile from my apartment most nights and studying at Barnes and Noble so that I could access their Wi-Fi.

Some nights, especially the evenings where I had to write a paper or take an online test I would have to study outside in the dark right outside of Barnes and Noble because they closed before I was finished. I needed to access their Wi-Fi so that I could upload my paper and submit it before the midnight deadline. Often, I would sit out there in the rain, covered by the awning from the store. I don't think I ever even thought about how dangerous it was out there at night all alone like that. I was in such a grind doing what needed to be done, on a mission to complete my degree.

My daughter LaTina was working and I lived over fifty miles from her so I did not get to see her often. I was always alone, I never had any company and I never made any friends. I did become pretty close with a couple of my coworkers but they had their own lives and except for one or two times we never did anything together outside of work. I also met an attorney. She was from Wisconsin and we became pretty close as well.

I never thought I would get to the point where I would consider taking my own life but moving to Atlanta, is the abyss where my life began to enter "The Valley." When I was in Wisconsin before I lost everything, I had everything. I was respected in my community as a strong, Christian business woman with a beautiful family. I had close connections with many of Milwaukee's dignitaries, we built a $450,000 home in Germantown, my husband and I both drove Lincoln Navigator's (his was black and mine was white), our daughters were all beautiful and intelligent, and we had a business and bank account to back it all up.

Although I was blessed with so much, I was very humble. After my ex-husband and I built our home I would still come home every day humbled in disbelief that God blessed our family so tremendously. To be honest, in hind sight it almost felt like I was just sitting back waiting to lose it all, so much so that it became my truth.

It wasn't until I moved to Atlanta that I realized I was that chick, you know the one who cared about social status and what people thought of me. It was my experiences in Atlanta that confirmed to me once again that moving there was a God thing. God knew that I would buckle under the ridicule and shame of losing the image of a strong, successful, black woman back home in Milwaukee. Not so much because of my self-perception, but more so because of how harshly people, even some of my own family, would judge me.

In Atlanta, no one knew who I "used to be." There was no pressure to stay on top and preserve the Patterson image, but what I did slowly begin to realize is that Atlanta was certainly a city of who's who. The crazy thing is people would see me and assume I was at this certain social status level and I was shamed into keeping my walls up because I refused to live my life as an imposter, pretending to be something or have something I did not have.

Honestly, those type of people were not the type of individuals I wanted around me. My motto was either except me for who I am or stay the hell away from me. I was so over the phony, wanna be pretenders that I would run across from time to time. I loved myself enough to know how toxic those types of individuals really are.

The truth is I was struggling tremendously in Atlanta. I worked for the Department of Family and Children Services food stamp program and I only brought home around $1600 per month and my rent was $1245 per month. I wasn't competitive in the job market yet because I had not completed my bachelor's degree. Even with the twenty-six years of experience I had owning and operating my preschool back in Wisconsin, without a degree it still was not enough to secure a good job.

As if that wasn't difficult enough, shortly after I got my job I developed sciatica and was bed ridden and disabled for about two weeks. Unfortunately, I had not been on the job long enough to have accumulated any sick leave so I did not get paid for my time off.

Due to those circumstances, I fell behind in my bills and began to pay my rent at the end of the month instead of the beginning of the month. I was getting eviction notices posted to my door every month and accumulated late fees in access of $400 every month. It was financially devastating.

My daddy, my daughter LaTina, and Michael were my life line. My daddy sent me money when he had it every month to make sure I ate and he paid my internet and house phone bill to make sure I had a way to communicate with my family. My daughter LaTina and Michael would help me whenever I needed anything else and my ex-husband even helped me a couple of times. Things were still very difficult for me. I got in situations several times where I had to ask people for help. I did not like doing it, but pride had no place in my life during that period. After losing everything in Wisconsin, the idea of losing my apartment and my job was not an option.

When I was doing well I helped a lot of people. I gave out several sizable loans and was never paid back and tried my best to help any and every one I knew was in need. I never judged anyone that needed my help. Unfortunately, it did not take me long to discover that I was the exception not the rule. I slowly began to learn that people do judge you, even if you helped them in the past. I think one of the most difficult moments for me was realizing that when I was reaching out for help, it shamed my children. I had reached a new level of feeling low and worthless.

Soon I became overwhelmed and more and more apprehensive about asking for help. There were times when I would go three or four days with no food and when I did eat I ate very little. Determined to stay strong I continued to pursue my degree. It was the only thing that made me feel validated and at that point my survival was predicated on my academic success. It was the one thing I felt I was doing right.

I had allowed shame to distance me from my daughters, my family, and my friends. I felt like I was in the middle of the ocean alone on a raft thousands of miles from any land. The breaking point was when I came home one day after work and my apartment door was kicked in. Someone had burglarized my apartment. They took my fifty-inch flat screen and my laptop. I was devastated. I needed my laptop for school. That was all I had in life and my television had become like a companion that kept me connected to the outside world. I could not afford to pay the $500 deductible on my renter's insurance policy.

I called my daughter crying profusely. She rushed over with my notebook laptop I had given to her when I moved there. I had forgotten all about it but in that moment, I once again felt God's love and protection. That was my graduating semester of my bachelor's program and there was no way I could have completed the semester without a computer since I was completely online in all of my classes.

My daughter took me home with her and would not allow me to go back to my apartment without a gun. I hated guns. That thing looked like a little monster to me. I kept it in the drawer of my nightstand by my bed and prayed I would never have to use it.

Shortly after the burglary I became overwhelmed and inundated with grief. It just felt as if everything was crumbling right from underneath me. I could feel myself being pulled into this black hole. I felt as if I was no longer in my body, lifeless, with no faith or hope. I literally felt as though I was having an out of body experience and I was watching myself from the outside looking in.

I tried to pray but I felt like God no longer heard me or loved me. My apartment felt so cold and lonely without my television and I no longer felt safe there. I don't know what came over me but I sat there in my room looking at a bottle of pain pills I had left over from my sciatica.

I picked the bottle up and opened it. I was tired. I am not talking about physical exhaustion. I was tired to my soul. There is no feeling worse than feeling like you have no hope and feeling alone. Honestly, in those moments I had convinced myself that my daughters and my family were better off without me. I felt like a burden.

I was so broken that I could not even open my mouth to ask God for help. I poured about fifteen pills in my hand and as I was about to put them in my mouth, suddenly the phone rang. It was my daughter LaNisha. She is going to be shocked to read this because I never told her this.

She said, "Hi mommy, I was just thinking about you and wanted to call you and tell you how much I love you and how proud I am of you. You have been through so much and look at you, about to get your degree and start your Master's program. You did it mommy. I love you so much."

I knew that someone was praying for me in those dark moments because right after my daughter LaNisha called me one by one all of my daughters had called to check on me by the end of the night. Last but not least, my daddy called me as he always did to check on me to make sure I was okay.

God knew my heart and He knew exactly what I needed to fight my way out of that black hole. Although my daughter

LaTina lived fifty miles away from me she sensed that I needed her. Her and her partner made a decision to move in the apartments directly behind me so that she could protect me and be more supportive.

I felt so affirmed in God's love for me. He showed me how much He was fighting for me and He came to my rescue by using the people I love most to pull me out of the darkness that consumed the black abyss that I was in. I felt God's love stronger than I had in months and I knew God was slowly nursing me back to His love and protection.

Oxygen Mask

If you want to soar in life you must first
learn to F.L.Y. (First Love Yourself)
                            ~Mark Sterling

The date was February 12, 2012. The year got off to a very difficult start for me. My sister was murdered right after midnight on January 2nd. I had just flown home for her funeral from Atlanta. A month later, I was flying back home to Wisconsin to lay my mother-in-law, Muriel Patterson to rest. I will never forget the phone call. I picked up the phone and it was my daughter LaNisha. She was hysterical and screaming at the top of her lungs that she was gone.

She kept screaming in a frantic voice, "Granny is gone mommy, she's gone! Help me, mommy please, Granny is gone!" My beloved mother-in-law Muriel Patterson died right in front of my two youngest daughters and my ex-husband.

I had to call my daughter LaTina and tell her of her grandmother's death. LaTina had previously scheduled a flight home the week Ma died to see her because she had not seen her in almost three years. Ma died on Sunday and LaTina's flight was scheduled for Thursday. I could see how broken my daughter LaTina's spirit was. She hadn't seen Ma in a couple of years and she took it especially hard.

I collapsed right there in the hallway of my oldest daughter's apartment. I flew to Houston that weekend for my grandson Zion's birthday party. I sat on the floor of my oldest daughter's apartment, stunned and lifeless. This could not be happening! All that I could think about is how much I wanted to be there for my two youngest daughters. They had been through so much already. I could not endure the vision that my babies had just witnessed their grandmother die of heart failure right in front of them. They were still dealing with the trauma of my leaving them to move to Atlanta.

Coming home to bury Ma was difficult enough but leaving my babies again to go back to Atlanta after everything they had been through was especially hard. I felt they needed me now more than ever. My daughter LaNisha was very strong and a college student but she had a very difficult time dealing with Ma's death. I could see the brokenness in both of my daughter's eyes when I left, but they were trying to be strong for me because they knew I didn't want to leave them. Leaving my babies just did not feel natural. I felt so helpless, like I failed my daughters.

When I arrived at the airport I sat down and broke down. The feeling of helplessness that consumed me was overbearing. I sat there and replayed the last few years of my life. I couldn't understand how things got to this point. I was so worried about how my daughters were going to move on without me after suffering such a traumatic loss. I wanted to put some normal back in their lives, but there I was sitting at the airport preparing to get on a flight that someone had to purchase for me because I couldn't even afford a ticket back to Atlanta. I felt overwhelmed with grief. I was sitting there silently praying for God to take this pain away from me.

I boarded my flight back to Atlanta like I always did, buckled myself in and began reading a book. The flight attendant began discussing the emergency protocols that are discussed on every flight. I heard them a thousand times and generally felt no need to look up and pay attention.

As I sat there reading my book I felt as if God was telling me to look up. I even sat there and thought, "For what?" But I kept hearing God's voice telling me to look up and pay attention. I placed my book on my lap and looked up. The flight attendant was just getting to the portion where she was instructing us on what to do when the cabin loses air pressure and the oxygen mask came down.

It was almost as if her voice reverberated throughout the entire cabin. My eyes closed in on her and she said, "Make sure you place the oxygen mask on yourself before helping someone else put theirs on." Tears started rolling down my face and I could not stop crying. God was using her to tell me that He was repositioning me so that I could be better for my family. See, I was used to being the one that everyone came to for help. I loved helping others, so much so that at times I put myself in harm's way. Please don't misconstrue what I am saying. It is okay to want to help others but when I thought about all the money that I lost over the years a great deal of it was spent helping others.

I remember the day I moved to Atlanta and my daughter picked me up from the airport. She actually mentioned how she watched me help so many people over the years and wanted me to recognize how I may have been too helpful because of where I was at that moment.

She said, "Mom it's okay to help people but not if it's going to hurt you." I remember being a little hurt by what she said, but in all honesty, sometimes the truth hurts. My daughter was right. On my way back to Atlanta all I could think about was what the flight attendant said. It was strange that the analogy came from a discussion about an oxygen mask because we can't live without oxygen. I felt as if God was telling me I am my children's lifeline and in order to be able to be there for them I must first take care of me. It may sound selfish, but in truth if I'm a mess then what good am I to my children? Ultimately, what affects me, affects them. We can't fool our children, they know when we're hurting.

As mother's we have an intrinsic need to nurture. Often that comes with the price of putting everyone and everything before ourselves. The price we pay leads to a pattern of dysfunctional relationships and people pleasing. Soon we become exhausted and burnt out. While that may sound like a noble quality, the truth is it is foolish. How can we help anyone if we are a mess ourselves? It's as though you are hanging on a cliff about to fall. You just end up taking people off the cliff with you.

The truth is all we are really doing is pulling our loved ones into our mess. As parents, we have a responsibility to build a strong foundation for our children to be successful and like it or not that starts with taking care of ourselves. It may sound selfish, but selfish or not it is necessary. It's been said that our children come first, I would contend that we come first. In taking care of ourselves we give our children the best version of who we are so that they can be the best version of themselves. At the end of the day when we're better, they're better.

"It Factor"

Elegance is not being noticed, it's about being remembered.

~Giorgio Armani

What is the "It Factor"? Through my lens, the "It factor" is the blessing that is disguised as a curse. I believe those of us who have it were born with it. The "It factor" is innate. It is not something you can buy, or put on, or pretend to have. You either have it or you don't. It may surprise many of you when I say that having the "It factor" not only requires confidence but it also requires humility.

You know the scene, we have seen it in so many movies. She walks into the room with the prowess of a lion. The moment she enters all eyes are on her. She moves with elegance and poise. Adorned with a magnetic energy that makes it feel as though time stands still the moment your eyes gaze upon her. Who is this woman? Her smile lights up the room, her beauty is infectious, and there is an internal energy that exudes from her that leaves you breathless.

You want to approach her but you feel in awe by her presence. She is confident but not arrogant. Educated but not condescending. She does not feel a need to be anything other than who she is. She is comfortable in her skin and feels no pressure to impress others. She is kind and does not esteem herself higher than anyone yet you find yourself feeling intimidated to approach her. What is it about this woman that draws you to her like a magnetic force field pulling you in?

It was only recently that I embraced that I have "it". You see having "it" may sound exciting and alluring but believe me beloved, often times it can be anything but exciting. For much of my life I would get dirty looks, people hating me for no reason, being harshly judged as being arrogant or conceited, and appearing unattainable or unapproachable. As a result, I often internalized these external circumstances and it ultimately effected my self-image and left me wondering what was wrong with me.

I have always had a difficult time building relationships with women. Quite often when I did I found them to be disingenuous. I am the type of person that pours her soul into her relationships be it my romantic relationships or my friendships. I am loyal to a fault and I have your back, so much so that it often leaves me in a sea of hurt and betrayal.

I admit I am not an easy person to get close to and with reason. I refuse to spend my life defending my character. Either your down for me or you're not. I have *zero* tolerance for BS, *PLEASE* know this!

On the other side of that there were times when people, complete strangers, would approach me and compliment me, not just on my looks but my presence. Often it came from women as well as men. After I lost everything it was hard for me to embrace "it". Prior to losing everything I never felt that I was one of those people that validated my self-worth based on what I had or that my self-worth was predicated on what people thought of me. Moving to Atlanta polarized my struggle in that area more than I cared to believe. Atlanta is truly a city of who you know and how people esteem you and whether you get in or stay out is predicated on your social status.

Honestly, at times my experiences were downright hilarious. I can remember so many times walking into a room and feeling as though the women were actually growling at me, giving me dirty looks as if I walked up to them and slapped them in the face for no reason at all. I mean I would have been in the room for all of five seconds and I would stand there laughing inside thinking to myself, "Are you kidding me right now, what the hell?!" I'll tell you what, you better have some confidence about yourself to withstand those situations. It can be extremely intimidating and challenging to deal with when it happens all of the time and can have a negative impact on your self-perception. If you're not careful before you know it you internalize it and make it about you.

In those moments, I would always think back to something my mother said to me when I was about nine years old. I had been having some problems with some girls at school. I told my mother about it and I will never forget what she told me. My mother looked me in the eye and said, "Honey you shouldn't worry when people talk about you, that's not the problem, worry when they stop talking about you."

There was this one girl in particular that would pick on me every day, she was so mean to me for no reason, but she was also much bigger and older than me. She was overweight and a lot of the kids at school picked on her, but I never did. My mother said, "Diana, there are people you will meet in this life that hate themselves. They wake their little raggedy butts up in the morning and they look in the mirror and say, somebody's gonna pay for this shit! Then, they take it out on you"

My mother and I laughed so hard I thought I was going to pee on myself. Oh, my goodness, that was so funny to me but momma made a very good point. Often when people hate us it is because they hate themselves and you mirror everything they *wish* they were and instead of being able to admit their admiration for us they turn it into hatred. Honestly, I don't think they understand it themselves. At the tender age of nine years old, I don't think I had the mental capacity to fully understood what my mother meant but as I matured and faced more and more of those experiences it became quite clear to me what my mother was trying to tell me that day.

The upside of the "It factor" is that it is God's affirmation to our self-worth and purpose. I personally believe that "it" is a gift bestowed upon us to be used as an instrument to bless and inspire others. After I lost everything and moved to Atlanta I felt lower than I had ever felt in my life. Here I was at the lowest point in my life, no car, working a job where I was living less than paycheck to paycheck, often unable to even feed myself, and at times feeling no sense of my self-worth and God used so many situations and circumstances in Atlanta to nurse me back to "it".

I remember a few "it" experiences in particular. One day I decided to walk to Target. I think I went to buy my daddy and my daughter LaTina a card because they had been so wonderful and so supportive through those difficult times. I was dressed in a pair of sweat pants and a t-shirt, a little eyeliner and no other make-up and feeling really detached that day for some reason. Target was about a mile and half from where I lived. It was really hot out that day so when I arrived at Target I had been sweating quite a bit and I thought I looked a hot mess, literally. I was feeling a little overwhelmed with work, balancing my classes, and the financial stress that I was experiencing.

As I walked through the store I could feel someone staring at me. Eventually this woman walked up to me and said, "I'm sorry I know you don't know me, but who are you?" I was confused by her question so I asked her what she meant. She said, "I swear I have never done this before, but you are so beautiful and your energy just pulled me in and I looked at you and said to myself, I have to find out who this woman is."

I was stunned because I felt so dark and alone that day and God used that woman to pull me out and shield me with His love. I thanked her for her compliment and we stood there and talked for a few minutes before going our separate ways.

There was another situation where I was on the train heading to work in the morning. I was reading a book and kept to myself as I always did on the train. I could feel someone looking at me. I never even looked up, but I could feel it like some sort of energy pulling me in. Suddenly, this young man stood up and walked next to where I was sitting. Initially he startled me but as he stood there he said in a very loud voice, "Lord, thank you for showing me this beautiful woman. I know I am not ready for this woman and I can't be for her the man you chose for her, but thank you for using this beautiful woman to show me the vision of what you are molding me and shaping me to have one day when you are finished with me." He tapped me on the shoulder and said. "Thank you, beautiful queen, thank you," and then got off the train at the next stop. This young man never asked me for my number or tried to talk to me, he just allowed God to use him as a vessel to extend a few words of kindness to restore something that was lost in me.

There was another incident on the train on my way to work one morning where a young man, a really nice looking one by the way, walked up to where I was sitting on the bus and started singing to me. I cannot remember the song he sang but the song was about a beautiful woman. After he sang the song, he kissed my hand and got off the train at the next stop. I just sat there amazed.

It was similar to the first situation. This young man didn't ask me for my phone number or ask me out. I just sat there in awe. As I sat there I began realizing there had to be something special about me and I asked myself what God wanted me to do with "it". I wanted to glorify and represent God with "it". He used "it" to nurse me back to knowing my self-worth.

Those were just a tiny handful of the many experiences I have had over the years. I still had a long way to go after suffering so much loss. God wanted me to see myself through His lens. God wanted me to realize that I should not validate my self-worth through the lens of my experiences and that where I was did not define who I was.

Each time I run into these encounters, and they happened often, I am so incredibly humbled and grateful. What I realize is this is God's awesome favor. I believe those of us that have been blessed with 'it' have a responsibility to use "it' wisely. The "It factor" is power and power is something that although very influential, should be handled with care. Having "it" is an opportunity to take something God gave us and use it to inspire others to be their best version of themselves

People who have "it" are often misunderstood. People make a lot of assumptions about those of us who have "it". Some of those assumptions are that our lives are perfect; we have it all together, we don't have any insecurities, we have perfect love lives, and can have anyone we want. Other common assumptions are that we esteem ourselves higher than others; we are difficult to approach, we only allow certain "types" of people in our lives, and the list goes on.

In truth, at least in my situation, I am a loner, I only have a couple of real friends, my love life has been complicated, and I have spent years at a time celibate and alone.

As I began to gain a few pounds it became especially difficult for me to embrace "it". The men my age would stare, but would seldom approach me and the baby boy playa's were aggressive and approached me because of the challenge, but it seldom appeared sincere. One of the most difficult challenges of having "it' was my relationships or dare I say the lack thereof, with women.

Honestly, there are times when I seriously feel like I am the most misunderstood woman on this planet, perhaps not in a literal sense but I am telling you, it can be overwhelming to constantly be made to feel like you have to defend your character to someone that has known you all of five seconds.

Baby, those days are behind me! I could care less what anyone thinks about me. Those individuals that take the time to put their preconceived notions about who or what I am enough to get to know me are often pleasantly surprised at how kindhearted, loving, and humble I really am. If they are *lucky* enough to become someone I care about, they find that they have a true friend for life, a ride or die, a friend that not only cares about them but will give you the shirt of her back.

Just like many others, I too have insecurities and fears. I crave companionship where the foundation is built on loyalty, vulnerability, honesty, and openness. I crave human connection as much as the next person. Often, like ninety percent of the time, when I go out to dinner, to a jazz concert or play, travel, or go to the movies, I am alone. My life is not glamorous or filled with men knocking down my door to get to me. So, the next time you see someone that has "it" be kind, approach them and get to know them for what's inside and put aside all of your assumptions and preconceived notions predicated on their external appearance. Draw into that beautiful energy that pulls you in and be open, if you do, I think you will be pleasantly surprised.

Sugar Land

I can't – believe - it's ~~over~~ a new beginning.
~Unknown

God has a way of making things happen and when it's a God thing it can happen in the strangest circumstances. I moved to Dallas, Texas to marry Michael, the man I thought I would spend the rest of my life with. Well, that didn't happen. Our relationship ended just six short weeks after I gave up my life in Atlanta to move to Dallas and be with him. There I was again, penniless, no job, no home, no plan, bruised and broken. Nothing but the empty fragments of a woman that was once so strong and confident had turned into a suspicious, phone snooping, email checking, insecure mess.

I left Dallas and moved to Houston to live with my oldest daughter LaToya and her family for a few months to try to figure out my life. My move to Houston was a God thing. The first couple of times I visited my daughter and her family in Houston I hated Houston and had absolutely no desire to live there. It was huge, hot, and the traffic was insane. My daughter LaToya had been begging me to move to Houston for a couple of years now, she knew things had been difficult for me but for me Texas was never on my radar.

God knew the only way He could get me to move to Texas was by way of Michael so God did what he had to do. My break up with Michael devastated me, especially after a failed marriage with my ex-husband, the only other man I ever truly loved. Michael and I had been best friends for years and I did not see the things that happened between us coming, but what I would soon see is that the move was all by God's design.

My daughter LaToya is my only child that has children. Her husband was her first and only love. I never thought back then that they would grow up, get married, and gift me with three of the most incredible grandchildren on the planet. I know every grandmother says that, but they really are. My daughter LaToya was pregnant with their third child when I moved to Houston. God knew with everything I had experienced over the last two years of my life I needed to be surrounded by my daughter and her family. LaToya is a wonderful mother and watching her with my grandbabies was something I needed to find my way back to some normal in my life.

A couple of months after I moved in with my daughter and her family, my other daughter LaNisha moved to Texas and started graduate school. It was a wonderful time for all of us. My youngest daughter LaShawna was considering moving to Texas as well. Things were beginning to feel normal in my life again and it was amazing. God knew that what I needed in order to heal was the love of my entire family and He was making it happen.

Having been alone as much as I was in Atlanta heightened my sense of needing the joy one feels in the presence of children and oh did my grandbabies shower me with love. It was perfect. My first semester of graduate school started that fall and I was soon in my own apartment. My daughter LaNisha moved in with me for a short time until she found her own apartment. I moved to a beautiful city in suburban Houston called Sugar Land and my move there was indeed sweet as sugar. A few months later my youngest daughter LaShawna moved in with me to attend college and pursue a career in modeling.

Things were a little rough for me in the beginning but God had lined up another divine intervention and it just so happened that the new pastor at my church was a close friend of my old pastor from Milwaukee. Pastor Joseph and his wife were a tremendous support system for me when I moved to Sugar Land and I could not have made it without their support and prayers. Pastor Joseph and his wife saw me through God's eyes and God used my family and Pastor Joseph and his wife to help birth something back in me that I had lost.

Soon I was hired by the State of Texas Department of Family and Protective Services as an investigator for Fort Bend County Child Protective Services. Michael gave me his truck when I moved to Houston and it wound up being a tremendous blessing because there is no way that I would have been able to accept the position if I did not have a vehicle. At the time, it appeared as though I was just taking the first job that came along but soon I discovered I was *chosen* for the position. As I looked back through my life, I found healing for circumstances in my own life through helping the precious children that I have been honored and chosen to protect.

Slowly, I could see God breathing the life back in me like a person receiving CPR and it felt amazing. Four semesters later, one of the happiest days of my life was approaching. I had completed my Master's degree in Administrative Leadership/Adult Continuing Education from the University of Wisconsin-Milwaukee. Completing my degree completely online was challenging and trying to navigate graduate school while working for CPS was almost impossible.

I do not have regular hours with CPS and the work required to protect the children we serve required many days where I worked late into the night and still had to go home and study for hours, sometimes trying to function on only one to two hours sleep. It was difficult and soon began to take a toll on my health. I ended up hospitalized a couple of times due to stress and other health related issues but I did not let that stop me.

It was spring 2015 and I was preparing for my graduation from graduate school. I was still struggling but I wanted to fly home to Milwaukee to walk across that stage. I poured my soul into that degree and felt so validated and amazing. I was so upset because I just did not have the finances to fly home and participate in my graduation ceremony. My daughter LaTina offered to fly me home, but I did not let her. One night I was on the phone with my cousin Carleton who lived in Beaumont, Texas, about two hours away. I told him about my graduation and he insisted on buying my plane ticket home. He said there was no way he was going to let me miss such a special day. I cried like a baby when I got off the phone. It felt amazing.

The day had come and there I was in Milwaukee, Wisconsin preparing to receive my Master's degree. I was so happy but there was another part of me that was empty. None of my daughters were able to attend my graduation because we were all bouncing back from what happened to our family and trying to get back on our feet. I reflected back on the time when I was earning a six-figure salary and it would have been nothing for me to fly every one of them home and pay for hotels for everyone and there I was only there because of the kindness of a family member.

I stood there in line waiting for them to call my name. My daddy, brother, aunts, uncles, nieces, Michael, my best friend, sister, and my two sister-in-laws were all there to support me. I knew my daughters were watching from a livestream but somehow it didn't feel right. After everything I had been through this moment meant so much to me. When they called my name, the tears flowed down my cheeks. I felt such pride as I walked across the stage. The celebration afterwards was nice but all I could think about is how much I wished my daughters, my grandchildren, and their families could have shared that day with me. I thought about my mother and how proud she would have been of me that day and in the end, it was all bittersweet.

After all the excitement of the day calmed down and I was finally alone I reflected on everything I had experienced over the last four years of my life. I vowed that day that I would do everything in my power to rebuild a strong financial foundation for my children and was committed to doing what I had to do to see it manifest. I never again wanted finances to interfere with my family's ability to share beautiful experiences together ever again.

Unlovable

"They only see your shell, they could never tell what you really feel inside. The happy lady they see they expect you to always be, but from them the truth you hide. Your smile is just a stain sitting on top of your pain, you need to rise above. My mama taught me ladies deserve respect and nothing less. All You Need is Love."

~From Frank McComb's Debut CD "Love Stories-2000"

I remember the first time I heard the lyrics from my favorite artist, Frank McComb's Love Stories cd. It touched my soul so deeply. His lyrics captured the essence of my life and my experiences. My love life has been complicated and lonely at best. I have only had a few relationships, but the outcomes for me were never good and the only two men that I ever loved hurt me tremendously. For me those fairytale endings were just that, fairytales. My friendships with women have not been much different.

My life has been a series of many experiences that at times left me feeling unlovable. As bad as that sounds there is nothing worse than losing faith to the point that you no longer believe that God loves you. Yes, I said it, there was a time in my life that I felt as though God did not love me. Not because

I felt God judged or abandoned me, but because I lost faith in myself and worse, I lost faith in God.

There are experiences that happen to us that draw us into a black hole. It is a place that is cold, dark, and barren. You can be surrounded by loved ones and friends and still feel alone, like no one *sees* you. It's as though you are standing in the middle of a crowd screaming at the top of your lungs, "HELP ME!" and no one hears you. You exist in a sea of brokenness and despair and just like the true characteristics of a black hole each subsequent negative experience pulls you in deeper and deeper. You exist in a state of nothingness, numb. You no longer feel anything, and you are just a shell of a person as if your soul has left your body.

As far back as my childhood I have experienced things that were extremely painful. I was not raised as a Christian, but I was raised to be a good person and to care about others. I had a firm belief in the notion that we have a responsibility to give back to our communities and I never wanted to see anyone hurting. In spite of the many challenges that I faced as a young person, I always seemed to manage to see the light. It was not until my mother died that I saw the world through a different lens and it became more and more difficult to balance the good and the bad experiences.

At some point, I began to validate my self-worth based on the things that were happening to me instead of who I was.

What's worse is that I felt so unloved that my prayer life became stagnant and I did not have the capacity to see myself through God's eyes. This my love, is dangerous territory. I thought I would never consider committing suicide but I have gotten to a point where I was in such a dark place that the idea of taking my life and pulling myself out of that pain felt almost comforting. This is where our relationship with God becomes critical.

If Satan were to have his way he would want us to believe that our spiritual foundation is nothing but a lie. We are placed in circumstances that eat at the very core of our spirit and exhumes every ounce of hope from us until we check out on life. For many it may not happen in a literal sense, but they may check out by detaching themselves from everyone and everything that fuels life and hope into them. Others live a pretentious life, walking around living their lives as if it were a masquerade ball, hiding behind their true selves, becoming people pleasing empty souls.

The residuals of feeling unlovable is that we sabotage every blessing God brings to us. God says in his word, "As he thinketh in his heart, so is he." Proverbs 23:7. As a result, our life becomes a self-fulfilling prophecy of what we believe about ourselves. We find ourselves pushing the people that love us away. We lose the capacity to believe that we deserve to be happy and internalize it in ways that are self-destructive.

We lose our vulnerability and are shamed into believing that we are unworthy and in essence, this becomes our truth.

God never intended for any of us to live our lives in this way. He instilled in each of us the resources we need to overcome adversity. He promised us that He would never put more on us than we can bear. Losing faith obstructs our ability to see our light. We become consumed with self-hatred and we lose the ability to believe that we are worthy of life's blessings.

I have been molested, beaten, betrayed, judged and misjudged, broken down to nothing and I am still standing. Some people look at me and assume my life is this fabulous adventure where I am surrounded by people that adore me, where men are knocking themselves over to get me, where there is never a dull moment, when in truth, I only have two true friends, a family that has loved me beyond my pain and nursed me back into the light, and most days I sit at home alone.

Unlovable is a state of being that was never intended for any of us. God sends us constant reminders through our experiences that we are loved and we have purpose. If we make a choice to exist in the darkness then we become victims of life's circumstances instead of conquerors on a mission to live our life in God's divine purpose. God's will for our lives is to hold on to His promise. God wants us to be happy and filled with joy. It's there right in front of us, all we have to do is embrace it.

I made a conscious decision not to include much information in this book about my relationships. We cannot allow the things that happen to us or the way people treat us when we are involved with someone become our self-perception. We tend to over analyze the circumstances that happen when we feel we are mistreated. We take on the responsibility of the other person's actions as though we caused them to mistreat us and that somehow it is our obligation to fix them.

We've all been there, you know that moment we gaze across the room and there he or she is, your person, your one. The planets align and gravity pulls you together, you thrust yourself into a relationship and hit the ground running. You found them, your happily ever after, or are they? It disturbs me how in this day and age of hooking up, few people take the time to get to know one another and build a strong foundation of friendship before getting physical with one another. When a person falls in love with your spirit and your character they are much more likely to stay with you. Relying on your beauty, body, money, or social status to keep someone around is a recipe for disaster.

One of my favorite scriptures in the bible is found in Proverbs 4:23, it says, "Above all else, guard your heart; for out of it flows the issues of life." God holds us responsible for our hearts. Although, we cannot control what others do to us, we are in *complete* control of what we do about it. At some point, we have to take full responsibility for our happiness and our lives and stop allowing another person's rejection or mistreatment make us feel low, unattractive, unworthy, and unlovable.

What I have learned and believe about love is the person that God has designed for you will have the heart to love you and the eyes to *see* you. What I mean by *see* you is love you unconditionally, flaws and all. I believe that if a person is not meant for you God will not give them the eyes or the heart to give you what you need to feel safe and secure to love that person because they are not the one He chose for you. We have to learn to let go and trust the process. What I know about God is when He says no, He means no.

I often tell women that *we* teach men how to treat us by the way we treat ourselves and the things we accept from them. If we want a man to be good to us, we have to be good to ourselves. Some of us want a prince when all we are presenting is a frog. If we want a king then we have to believe and present ourselves as queens.

Losing everything was an awakening for me. It was a very difficult but necessary process that I needed in order to live authentically. I am still rebuilding my life and I am still not involved with anyone, but I do know what I deserve and I am willing to wait on God's timing to have it.

In My Daddy's Arms

My father gave me the greatest gift anyone could give another person. He believed in me.
~Jim Valvano

I have always believed a child's first impression of God comes from their earthly father. Fatherhood for many can be a beautiful experience. Becoming a parent is one of the most difficult, challenging, and rewarding experiences one will ever encounter. It's one thing to plan children, it's another to be sort of thrown into parenting left to figure things out as we go. In truth, that's what we are all doing as parents, figuring it out as we go. There is no perfect or golden recipe for parenting. How we raise one child may not work for another. Parenting requires emotional intelligence, patience, a sense of humor, courage, empathy, self-awareness, and a lot of love.

I wrote this chapter as a tribute to my father, Joseph Horne Jr. By societies standards my father is technically my stepfather but in truth my father is no stepfather, he is my daddy and I could not love a man more than I love him. I use the term daddy to describe my daddy because for me it is a term of endearment. Unlike many I am blessed to have a man that met me at tender age of five years old and made a choice to love me and raise me as his own. It is one thing to be raised by a man that birthed you but to be raised and loved by a man that chose to love you is something very special.

My daddy is the first man I ever loved. Our relationship was not perfect, especially during my adolescent years when I was dating Quintin, my oldest daughter's father. My daddy is a very handsome, charismatic, wise, and caring man. I have learned a great deal from him over the years. He does not have a college degree, but don't let that fool you, he is very intelligent and seems to know a great deal about many things. His intrinsic nature is that he is a giver. I don't ever recall seeing my daddy walk away from anyone that was in need, often putting his own needs last.

My daddy always saw the best in me, even when I didn't see it in myself. As a teenager, I disappointed my parents at times, especially when I got pregnant with my oldest daughter. I ran track in middle school and held a couple of state records. My daddy had aspirations of sending me to an Olympic summer camp to prepare me for the Olympics the summer that I got pregnant. I think my daddy took it hard when I got pregnant because he saw such a bright future for me. Telling my parents I was pregnant was one of the hardest things I ever had to do. My daddy did not speak to me for a long time after I got pregnant but eventually he came around, I knew he would. He knew my potential and was aware of the challenges

I would face in life as a single teen parent. Neither of my parents would have chosen that path for me.

I moved to Milwaukee after I graduated from high school. My parents divorced before I left Madison and for a while I did not talk to my daddy often, not because there was anything wrong in our relationship but more so because that was back in the days when we had to pay for long distance phone calls. I am really throwing my age out there now.

My daddy has always been there for me when I needed him, but after my mother died our bond grew even closer. It meant the world to me, more than any expression of words could convey. He could sense how much I needed him during that time and he was determined to give me what he felt in his heart that I needed which was just to be there for me. He could have easily said, "Oh well that's not my daughter and she is an adult now after my mother died," but instead he poured himself into being there for both me and my brother in any way that he could.

My daddy is my greatest sounding board and he just gets me. He has this way of nurturing me through my pain no matter what I'm going through. Just the sound of my daddy's voice brings me to a good place when I'm hurting and I still feel like a little girl in his presence. My daddy makes me feel safe in a world that at times consumes us with fear.

There is no greater gift than to have been blessed to have someone that can love you past your pain, looks beyond your flaws, and builds you up with their love. For me that's my daddy. After I lost everything my daddy nurtured me back to loving myself again. He called me every day when I was in Atlanta and on a small fixed income he sacrificed and regularly sent me money to make sure that I was eating and had internet so that I could complete graduate school. He valued the things that were important to me and he NEVER judged me.

My daddy did not have all of the answers but what he did have is what I needed most, unconditional love. I see and feel God's love for me through my daddy and I feel safer in this world because of it.

I See Color

And, then she decided to dance with her soul.
~Tara Catalano

When we are living a valley experience our world may appear dark, cold, grey, and colorless, with no hues of light. We become consumed with darkness as if we were dropped into a deep canal and no one knows we are there. We are lifeless and alone with no energy to pull ourselves into the light. My love, no matter how alone you feel in those moments it is imperative that we hold on to our faith in God. It is that faith that propels us into the light. God uses love as the harness that shields us from dying in the darkness.

My journey to write this book started five years ago with an occasional journal that catapulted into this book project in which I let down my shield of vulnerability to share pieces of my life with you. I had no idea at the time that God was using this journey, this project of writing this book to transport me into the light. Reliving some of the experiences that I have shared with you at times felt as though I was being pulled back into that abyss of darkness, but soon what I realized is that it was God's way of affirming that I was never alone and He never abandoned me.

In those darkest moments where I saw no color God used love through the circumstances and the people around me to bring color back into my life. Now my life is an ocean filled with hues of orange, teal, blue, yellow, purple, and gold. I am dancing in a shower of color that affirms my purpose. My redemption has given me a new perspective, a new lens in which I see the world, a world in which I embrace adversity and know it is there to strengthen me, knowing God will never put more on me than I can bear.

The opportunity to write this book does not make me better than anyone. What is does is open up an opportunity for me to create a platform to connect with people and inspire them to be the most authentic true version of themselves. The day I received my Master's degree for me was humbling because what I realized is nothing about my character had changed. I was still Diana with some knowledge sprinkled on top.

I believe that wisdom and knowledge are not the same. We can receive knowledge by furthering our education or through professional development. Wisdom however, comes from our experiences and what we do with that experience. It is sad commentary that many who achieve their degrees, a promotion or a substantial rise in their socioeconomic status suddenly esteem themselves higher than others. We are chosen into greatness to inspire, encourage, and support others, not to abuse our power.

Tears of joy and redemption are flowing as I write this chapter. God has affirmed my resilience and strength. Writing this book has given me redemption and restored everything that was lost in the valley. During my journey, I learned to embrace life's adversities and behold its beauty. You see my love, adversity too has a purpose.

I thought back to Christ's darkest hour when he was on the cross paying the ultimate debt for our sins and he cried out, *"My God, My God, why hast thou forsaken thee?"* Matthew 27:46. Our suffering is not in vain and if we could take a moment to look around and enjoy the beauty in the valley our redemption will then become a greater gift than we could have ever foreseen.

The ascension from the valley experience is about looking within yourself and seeing God in you. It drives us to tap into our inner souls and reclaim our identity that was placed in us before we were in our mother's womb, an identity that affirms our greatness and our connection to this universe and to God. I now see the mountain through a new lens. I see beauty in both the valley and the mountain's peak. The mountaintop no longer appears cold and barren. I have clarity and a renewed understanding of what it means to be up there alone with God.

I want to thank each of you for extending your hearts to me and caring enough to take some time out of your very precious and busy lives to engage in my life. My prayer is that this book will be an affirmation to your life and a testament that you are not alone in your journey to live, not to exist, but to live. I am here with you and together we can climb that mountain of redemption and embrace the journey that got us there and learn how to embrace life's valleys.

Lastly, I would like to share with all of you some lessons I've learned along the way. My prayer is that there is something here that will feed your soul and cultivate authentic living for each of you.

What I've learned:

- In life, you will meet three kinds of people; moment, season, and lifetime. Pray for discernment of who to let in, when to let them in, and when to let go. They each have a unique purpose in our life.
- You are your greatest resource.
- We get one shot at this life, no do-overs. Have fun, be kind, and get it right the first time.
- We can't live perfect lives, but we can serve a perfect God
- Love is not complicated, we are.
- Angels are not some biblical myth. They are real.

- Happiness is a choice.
- Humility is a prerequisite to connection.
- Time is one of life's most precious commodities. Be careful how you spend it and who you spend it with.
- Teach your children that they are not products of their environment, they are products of their choices.
- Embrace your uniqueness. It's the most beautiful thing about you.
- You can't move forward and look backwards at the same time. If you don't believe me, try it.
- Be present, not just in the room, present.
- Forgiveness is freedom (this includes self-forgiveness).
- Don't have regrets. They are just lessons.
- Hurt people, hurt people.
- Above all else, love yourself; it is the greatest gift we can give to our loved ones.
- God uses the universe to whisper to us. It's up to us to listen.

My Legacy
Love Letters to My Daughters

Someday when the pages of my life ends, I know that you will be one of my most beautiful chapters.
~Unknown

The bond between mother and daughter is as timeless and as infinite as the universe. It can be as gentle as a baby's breath and as tumultuous as a tsunami. A mother's daughter is a reflection and extension of her soul. What we invest in them will encompass our true essence and when we transcend into the next life our legacy will live on through them.

I was very careful to protect my children when I was writing this book. I am a very kind woman but when it comes to my children I am like a fierce lioness protecting her cub. If you ever want to see me out of my element, mess with one of my babies. My decision not to include certain aspects of my life was largely to ensure that the focus was on what really matters.

I would not be here today if it weren't for my four beautiful daughters. God gifted me with each of them for a different purpose in my life. LaToya is my spiritual confidant and sister. LaTina is my protector and counselor. LaNisha is my mother (laughing). LaShawna is my joy.

This chapter is a tribute to my daughters, my guardian angels, the loves of my life. My love for all of you surpasses time.

LaToya

My beautiful and precious LaToya, on March 21st, 1981, my entire life changed. I fell in love with you while I carried you in the womb. Still a child myself, we grew up together. I had no clue what I was doing when you were born. I was afraid but somehow, I knew we would figure this life out together. Your presence gave me beauty I never knew and the love you gave me affirmed me in ways that are indescribable.

Watching you raise my grandchildren and pour your soul into each of them gives me so much joy. I don't only see you and your husband when I look at them, I see me, my mother, my grandmother, and I see the Edwards legacy live on. There is no greater gift a child can give her parents than to give them grandchildren.

I have watched you blossom into an amazing, virtuous woman, mother, wife, business woman, educator, and prayer warrior. The honor of being able to call you my daughter is truly one of my life's greatest blessings. You have seen me go through so much and you prayed me through some of the darkest moments in my life. You held me up, believed in me, and encouraged me through times when I felt alone. When I look at you I see a reflection and extension of me.

As I watch you pour yourself into children through your work it restores something that I lost when I closed my preschool. Seeing you create such beautiful creative arts programs with the children in your summer camp gives me hope that someday that preschool of the arts that I always wanted will manifest through you. You have taken that intrinsic gift and love for children to help children reach greatness. There are no words to describe how proud I am of you LaToya, no words.

LaTina

My beautiful, precious, LaTina. March 23rd, 1986 was one of the most memorable days of my life. You were born a little over a month after my mother died and you were God's gift sent to heal some of the brokenness from that loss.

By the time I had you, I was beginning to figure this mother thing out. The instant I laid my eyes on you after you were born I knew there was something incredibly special about you. Although you were just a newborn, I saw so much love in your eyes for me and my love for you was as infinite as time. You were so precious and fragile. You would cry the instant you even thought I was walking out of the room.

You have been protective of me since you were a baby and the love you have poured out to me over the years has given me the blessing of knowing how it feels to be truly loved and protected. You saw the best in me when I did not see it in myself. You were always there to encourage me and you helped me see myself through your eyes and the eyes of God.

You never allowed me to give up on myself or to check out on life. Watching you grow up into an extremely beautiful, intelligent, courageous, driven, kind, and caring woman has gifted me with an affirmation that I did something right when I doubted myself. You are in tune with me and at times you know even better than me what's best for me and you never allow me to settle.

Raising you has truly been one of my life's greatest honors. During a period when I did not think I wanted to live you pulled me back into the light. You continue to protect me and your love for me is reaffirmed daily through your actions. You have taken the circumstances you've been through and used them to help you soar. Now you are beginning to live your dream and your business is about to flourish. To say that I am proud of you is not merely enough to describe the joy you give me by living your purpose and manifesting your passion. I am so honored to be the woman God chose to be your mother.

LaNisha

LaNisha my precious baby, I had no idea how much my life would change on May 7th, 1989, the day you entered this world. You were tenacious straight out the womb and when you wanted something you did whatever was necessary to get it and that has not changed over the years. Your illness helped the two of us to form a very special bond. That feeling of how much your life depended on me gave me something I needed through some very dark and difficult times in my life.

I'm not sure at what point it happened but somewhere between puberty and adulthood you became the mother and I became the child (laughing). Your accomplishments have affirmed so much about my life and about my commitment to raise you and your sisters in a way that honored our family's legacy. You never allowed your illness to dictate your life or your future. I look up to you for strength and you have always given it to me straight no matter what, the same way my mother did when I was young.

The way you have fought to not only stay alive but to excel and live well has encouraged me to do the same. You have given me so much joy and love, and you saw me through a lens that gave my life meaning. In caring for yourself enough to fight for your dreams and never allow your diabetes to beat you, taught me to fight for myself.

Watching you grow up into a beautiful, highly educated, driven, kind, giving, and loving wife, stepmother, and woman is the affirmation I need to know I did something right and for that I am forever grateful.

I cannot describe how much joy it gives me to raise a child that has been so committed and accomplished in spite of the challenges you face. Your courage and ambition to never give up gave me the fight I needed to survive through the valley.

LaShawna

LaShawna, my precious little snuggle bunny. It was by design that you were born on Valentine's Day February 14th, 1994. From the first moment that I held you and looked into those big beautiful brown eyes I felt so much love. You are God's expression and manifestation of love in action. You have always wanted to be close to me and near me. You cultivate love to those around you and everyone feels it.

You bring light into my world when I am down and you go out of your way to make sure your mommy feels loved and adored. When I look at you I see myself when I was young all over again. You constantly remind me of my beauty and you remind me to embrace it. As you excel and build a life for yourself, I am reassured that you will be okay because you are determined to survive no matter what life throws at you.

Your flawless beauty, strength, love, ambition, kind and giving heart are the attributes that I admire and love. You light up the room every time you walk in and bring an energy to the room that's infectious. You embody every attribute necessary to be a top model one day and I can't wait to see you grace the cover of magazines. It has been one of my life's greatest joys to raise you. I am truly humbled and honored to have been chosen as your mother.

You are my youngest child and I know at times you feel like you have four mothers instead of one but please know your sisters and I protect you because we love you. With each year that passes I watch you blossom into this amazingly beautiful and driven woman, and I am so very proud to proclaim to the world that you are my daughter, my baby, my love.

About the Author

Diana N. Patterson is a certified life coach and personal development consultant, child advocate, leadership consultant and trainer, educator, motivational speaker and author. Diana is determined to take her life experiences and use them to assist others in creating a life where they maximize their potential.

Everything Grows in the Valley is Diana's first literary composition and was written to inspire her readers to see adversity through a new lens, one in which they can overcome any obstacle that life brings them.

For information on booking an inspiring and powerful speaker, to schedule leadership trainings for your organization, or for booking a life coach session see information below:

Diana N. Patterson M.Ed.

DNP Consulting and Life Management

DianaPatterson@DNPLifeconsulting.org

facebook.com/DNPLifeConsulting

Instagram: @DNPLife

DNPLife.com

Milton Keynes UK
Ingram Content Group UK Ltd.
UKHW020731220923
429186UK00015B/872

9 781088 289693